WALKING
IN THE
SALZKAMMERGUT

Vorderer Gosausee

CONTENTS

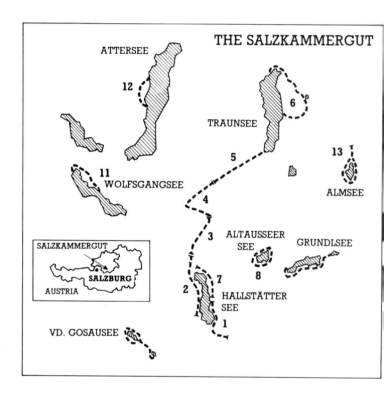

INTRODUCTION

The Salzkammergut - Austria's Lake District - contains some of the most spectacular scenery and some of the most delightful walking country in the whole of Austria.

Astonishingly, it remains little known to most English-speaking ramblers. Guidebooks in English which mention the region are few and far between and are generally superficial or even misleading. Perhaps part of the problem arises because it is not easily identifiable on a map, being composed of three Austrian Länder or federal states: Upper Austria the greater part, Land Salzburg and Styria in western Austria and having southern Germany (Bavaria) as its western boundary. Yet given the love and affection in which British people hold their own Lake District, it is surprising that many more have not discovered a region so very different yet with so many similarities in the Eastern Alps, which offers opportunity for every kind of walking from the toughest mountaineering to lakeside strolls.

The purpose of this book is to provide an introduction to what we believe is one of Europe's loveliest areas, one which, unlike many areas of the Alps, is admirably suited to the novice walker. So many people we have spoken to who have taken walking holidays in various parts of Britain, in the Lake District, the Yorkshire Dales, Cornwall or even Scotland have hesitated to plan a walking holiday in Austria, worried that once in the high Alps they will soon face routes which in steepness and difficulty are beyond their ability. This book is intended to remove such fears, being a collection of walks in the Salzkammergut which are in essence 'Holiday Rambles' -relatively easy, and for the most part straightforward routes which can be completed in less than a day, and in some cases a morning or afternoon, to allow for sightseeing in an area which is so culturally rich.

Only in one case - Walk Six - has a route been included which could be classified as strenuous, with a short but slightly tricky section, and this for reasons of continuity. Even the more difficult part of this route can easily be avoided. Otherwise each day can be made part of a holiday in which there is adequate time not only to enjoy some fine rambling but also to spend time seeing some of the great natural features or cultural attractions of the area.

Each walk is based on public transport. We assume that the majority of visitors to the Salzkammergut will come out by plane or even train rather than car and therefore not have a car available. Public transport in this region is so excellent that few places are inaccessible by train, bus (mainly the yellow Austrian Postbuses) or even boat, and each one of these walks has been planned to fit in with the public transport network from such popular centres as Bad Ischl, Bad Aussee, Gmunden or even St. Wolfgang.

The picturesque Salzkammergut railway which leaves the main Salzburg-Vienna line at Attnang-Pucheim for Stainach-Irdning goes through the heart of the Salzkammergut and provides the core transport network for the region. The buses and boats which link to this railway service will get you to and from everything in this book. If you do have your own or a hire car available, provision is made to link back to or from a parked vehicle in every case.

Cable-cars were not included in the public transport links even though they are a particularly useful means of transport for the walker because we felt that as this isn't a book of high level and mountain routes, we didn't want to lead people into areas where sudden changes of weather can cause problems and where long descents can be every bit as difficult and tiring as ascents. But if you do hit a spell of hot weather in the region and want to escape to cool mountain summits, several superb opportunities exist.

The book is organised in three parts. Part One we have called 'Before your Trip' and gives you a brief background to this fascinating region and its remarkable history which in so many ways the walks will explore, as well as providing you with some practical information to help plan your trip and get the most out of your visit. It will help explain some of the

Salzkammergutbahn

things you will see on the walk and hopefully provide an introduction to this very special part of Austria.

Part Two is devoted to walking the 'Salzkammergut Way' - our purely unofficial name for a suggested 80km long distance route through the centre of the Salzkammergut from Obertraun to Gmunden, much of it along the historic 'Soleleitungsweg' - the ancient saline pipeline from Hallstatt to the Traunsee which, because it runs parallel to the Salzkammergut Railway line, can be walked in easy day or half day stages between stations and halts (or boat landing stages).

Part Three takes a selection of seven other 'lakeland' walks in different parts of the Salzkammergut, all with an emphasis on lakesides with woodland shelter for hot summer days (or shelter on wet days) to give an introduction to the remarkable variety of scenery provided by the Austrian Lake District. Several of these can be combined with boat trips on the lakes themselves, providing a very civilised way of enjoying the scenery.

Gmunden - Traunsee Walk 6

All walks offer opportunity for quite excellent food and drink in sometimes surprisingly remote places - one of the real delights in store for anyone who has yet to walk in mountain Austria.

In researching and in writing this book we have been given considerable assistance by Herr Günter Wacek of the Salzkammergut Regional Tourist Office who has both given generously of his time and expertise and provided us with invaluable help and sources of information which for visitors to the region would have been difficult or impossible to find. We are enormously grateful to him for this generosity which to us symbolises the kindness and warmth that ramblers will find throughout the Salzkammergut. Needless to say any mistakes in the text are entirely our own.

PART ONE - BEFORE THE TRIP

THE SALZKAMMERGUT - AN EMPEROR'S PARADISE

'An earthly paradise!' this was the instinctive response of the Emperor Franz Joseph I, a personality not normally given to expressing himself in superlatives, when he wrote to his mother about the feelings Bad Ischl and the area around it awakened in him. It was a deeply felt tribute to the beauty of the landscape, its dazzling series of lakes, game-stocked woodlands, high alpine meadows and rugged mountains.

Two other monarchs some centuries earlier, however, saw the Salzkammergut rather differently. Its geographical position with no clearly defined border between Bavaria in South Germany and Austria, had fomented such political discord between the two countries in earlier times that Maximilian I saw it as a divisive 'stumbling block' in the way of improving relations between the two nations. More damningly, the region was also accused of being a continual thorn in the flesh of its Habsburg rulers. In the early seventeenth century Emperor Ferdinand saw it as a 'hotbed of disloyalty and rebellion' in spite of tight imperial controls and geographical and political constraints. It was no accident that Protestantism took deep root here as opposed to the rest of largely Catholic Austria. All the power of the Catholic church supported by the ruling caste and many punitive measures largely failed to eradicate it as the number of evangelical churches at, for example, Hallstatt, Gosau and Bad Goisern, still testify. It also took two attempted Turkish invasions of Austria to help bring this rather independent spirit of the Salzkammergut to heel.

The imperial theme is continued by the very name of the Salzkammergut itself as the term literally means Salt Chamber Estate, in other words a salt-producing area which was owned and administered by the Austrian crown, which derived its revenue directly from salt mining and salt refining - though the name Salzkammergut seems to have only come into use in 1656.

Millions of years ago the region now known as the Salzkammergut was covered by a great salt sea and as the salt concentration in the subterranean basins increased, the basins in time dried out. Later rock movements from within forced the Alps upwards and lifted the salt levels. The resulting rock mixture of sandstone, anhydrite, gypsum, clay and crystalline salt, can be seen in the salt mines of Hallstatt and Bad Ischl and Bad Aussee. Centuries ago early man had discovered the usefulness of salt as a flavour and later preservative, and had indeed evolved a number of techniques to produce it. The prehistoric salt miner had to tunnel through the rock with primitive tools in order to reach the salt. This was later abandoned by the Celts in favour of loosening or dissolving the salt in water. They evaporated the water with the help of stones heated in a wood fire and obtained pure salt. Later still, special buildings with heated cauldrons or giant vats were built (Pfannhäuser), in order to refine the salt. The name Pfannhäuser is still in use today for the highly sophisticated machinery and bore devices now used. The town of Pfandl outside Ischl is another reminder of the Pfannhäuser and their sites.

What makes the story particularly astonishing is the obvious difficulty of the terrain with its chains of mountains and lakes and swift-flowing and often treacherous rivers - not the easiest of places to colonise. The Salzkammergut consists of lake and mountain landscape with the Dachstein mountain range (at 2,996 metres the Dachstein is the highest mountain in Upper Austria) with its glaciers as its climax and the River Traun as its vital artery. Its landscape varies from flower-filled meadows and the high pastures of Alms, to pine or mixed woods, the cragged limestone of the Gosau range and the karst plateaux of the Totes Gebirge, bare of vegetation. Among the best known of the reputed 76 lakes of the Salzkammergut are the Hallstättersee ('See' is lake in German), Traunsee, Attersee, Altaussee, Grundlsee, Mondsee, Gosausee, Almsee and the Wolfgangsee (sometimes known as the Abersee) and each of them has a highly individual character.

The original area of the Salzkammergut included the land in the south of Austria up to the Hallstättersee, the Gosau area

Hallstatt

and the whole of the upper Traun valley to Ebensee. This was later extended to include the Aussee area and a whole additional chain of lakes, as the area became increasingly opened up to the tourist by the coming of the railways in the nineteenth century.

HALLSTATT AND ITS WHITE GOLD
The small town of Hallstatt in the centre of the Salzkammergut provides a key to the extraordinary history and diversity of this remarkable region, shaped as it has been by the exploitation of one major mineral - salt.

The picturesque little town so enjoyed by present day visitors clings to its prehistoric site on a narrow ledge between a thickly forested mountainside and the lake, its charming houses and close-packed streets concealing the story of its remarkable past. The name Hallstatt or 'Salt Town' gives the key to its former importance, the word 'hal' is a Celtic word meaning salt and is similar to the Greek word *háls* - not so surprising because there were close cultural links between the Illyrians, originally from Venice, and the Greeks. Not only Hallstatt, but also Hallein near Salzburg, Hall in Tyrol, Bad Hall near Linz and Schwäbisch Hall in Germany show a similar derivation.

It is thought that salt was mined at Halstatt about 1000 BC or at very least, use was made of the natural brine springs. As we progress to 900-500 BC and the period known as the Hallstatt Culture, we may ask ourselves why these Illyrian tribes people, followed by the Celts, should have settled in such an isolated spot at the mercy of dangerous river currents, avalanches and rock falls and how did it come about that such an amazing civilisation flourished here hemmed in by water and mountain with little space for even the most primitive dwellings? The answer is of course salt and salt mining; of enormous economic importance to Bronze and Iron Age man. Excavations in and around old mine workings on the hillsides above the town have uncovered miles of galleries, textiles, leather shoes, parts of wooden bowls, wedges used in mining, broken axes, burnt out torches and many more items of great archaeological interest.

Hallstatt's famous prehistoric burial grounds have yielded about 20,000 objects and in the eighteenth century the body of a still clothed Celtic miner or as he became known 'The Man preserved in the Salt' helped to enhance our knowledge further. Heart shapes chiselled into the underground rock have been discovered which seemed to have formed a pattern enabling an oval shaped rock fragment on each side to be knocked out and then the central salt layer with the help of wedges later to be chipped free. Remains of early ladders in the form of holes hacked regularly into the supporting walls of the tunnels and galleries with logs laid across have also been found. In the Hallstatt Heimat (Folk) Museum is a perfectly preserved conical carrying sack for rock salt made of goatskin with fur side outermost, stretched on wooden laths. It was so constructed that a comparatively light movement was needed to empty it. The miner's leather cap is also on display.

Light underground seems to have been obtained by bunches of wooden spills fastened together with fibrous string from the linden tree and these torches were probably held in the teeth while climbing. Longer lasting light would be given by metre-long spills of fir or pine fastened together. The objects in the Hallstatt graves include glass bowls and beads, and bronze objects suggesting an extensive trade with the Baltic and beyond. A superb sword with intricate ivory and amber decor-ation, daggers with goldleaf decor and brooches of great artistry show that salt - the white gold - meant wealth. Ceramics in striking patterns and stylised animals in bronze testify to a high standard of workmanship. An etching on a Hallstatt sword sheath shows two figures holding a winding wheel which may well have been used for pumping out water or brine. Bronze and Iron Age remains also indicate that clay cylinders were placed on the ground as stands for shallow pottery vessels filled with salt water. Fires were lit between the cylinders causing the water to evaporate and leaving a deposit of moist salt which could then be taken to containers of porous clay and dried.

The Celts from the west about the fourth century BC conquered the kingdom of Noricum and salt mining, together with copper and iron working, flourished with a high degree of craftsmanship as the museums of Hallstatt, Gmunden and Vienna all demonstrate.

The Romans who followed were clever enough not to kill the goose who laid their particular golden eggs and were able to co-exist for the most part peacefully with the Celts, overseeing the indigenous salt miners; the Roman period marking an era of increasing wealth and economic development. Ischl and Gmunden became administrative centres, and we discover, for example from a tablet in Ischl parish church inscribed by Secondinus, a Roman slave and administrator of the Ischl office, that the Celtic custom post at Ischl was in communica-tion with the Emperor's salt mines in Hallstatt and also seems to have had military protection.

Throughout the Middle Ages and till the mid-fourteenth century the Salzburg region and the Salzkammergut were locked in conflict over their respective salt rights, though there was plenty of salt for the Prince-archbishops of the Salzburg area at Hallein. In fact the latter were able to pay their soldiers from the proceeds of the salt mines as they continued their seemingly endless skirmishes with the Bavarians who were very near neighbours. It also enabled them to build and decorate, at a later date, churches and palaces in the full baroque architectural splendour of gold and marble. 'The white gold' brought power and influence to its possessors.

In the thirteenth century salt production increased in Hallstatt when Albrecht's widow Queen Elisabeth handed over twelve refineries in the town to burghers with sufficient capital in return for certain obligations, including military. You pass a plaque in the centre of Hallstat which indicates this story, whilst Hallstatt's two museums - Prehistory and Heimat (Folk) museums (open daily from April to end of September) contain major collections of archaeological and other remains from sites which are of European importance for what they tell us of early civilisations.

The salt was carried in rock or crystal form from Hallstatt to Gmunden along a route via Lauffen probably very similar to that used by Walks Two to Five in this book. Gmunden was the seat of the Salzamtmann, an official who supervised all matters pertaining to the mining, refining and sale of salt. Up till the later nineteenth century, the road from Gmunden only went as far as Traunkirchen so that salt had to go by boat down the River Traun and across the Traunsee. On the return trip various provisions such as cereals and wine were brought back by lake, river and packhorse way. They were taken by carriers known as the Traunreiters who followed the banks of the River Traun and a colourful modern mosaic describing their journeys can be seen high up on a wall on Pfarrgasse, one of the main shopping streets in Ischl. Walk Three uses a surviving section of the Traunreiters' Way along the side of the Traun.

Not until 1872 was there an extension of the public road as far as Ischl and Hallstatt itself could only be reached from the north on foot or on horseback by mountain track or footpath. Those who insisted on greater comfort could be carried by chairmen over the steep paths. An open chair of the type used can be seen in the Heimat Museum in Hallstatt and there is also an enclosed sedan chair which could be used for this

A Traunerl on the Hallstättersee

purpose. A wooden carrier strapped to a person's back can also be seen for carrying lumps of rock-salt over the mountains. A walk over the sometimes precipitous Soleleitungsweg (see Walk Two) *without* 20 kilos or so of rock strapped to your back will indicte the enormity of such an effort, which nevertheless was often carried out by women.

THE WORLD'S FIRST PIPELINE

Much of the salt carried from Hallstatt was by water - a cheap and practical mode of bulk transport - but navigation problems on the rapidly flowing River Traun and shallow parts of the lakes required the salt to be transported part way by packhorse or horses and carts till weirs and even a short stretch of canal - the Umfahrungskannal - were built which raised the water table a metre on the Hallstättersee and enabled boats to travel down to the Traunsee all the way along the River Traun from Ischl where there were wharfs close to the present day Goldenes Schiff Hotel. But between the Hallstättersee and Ischl goods had to be trans-shipped to waggons or baskets hauled by horses along the riverside tracks.

A special kind of shallow-bottom barge or gondola - the Traunerl - was devised to cope with loads along the lakes and shallow rivers, a traditional style still very much in evidence on the Salzkammergut lakes today. Use is still made of these boats, suitably decorated for the annual Corpus Christi processions on the lakes at Traunkirchen and Hallstatt. Originally the boats used to be sold after each trip down river, to save the return trip and raise income, but eventually timber shortages caused the barges to be pulled upriver by people and later horses.

None of these methods of transport were satisfactory, being slow and time-wasting, so in 1607 the world's first long-distance pipeline was completed, the Soleleitung ('Sole' means brine) to carry the salt in liquid form as brine along the 40 kilometres between Hallstatt and Ebensee. This wooden pipeline was constructed out of 13,000 hollowed-out tree-trunks, carefully joined together and sealed and laid on a superbly constructed shelf along the mountainside - the Soleleitungsweg. This route, now a footpath for most of its length, is used for most of all of three walks in this book, forming part of the Salzkammergut Way along the Traun Valley - Walks Two, Three and Five. The Soleleitungsweg is both a spectacular walking route and a superb piece of engineering and industrial history in its own right - still in use and adapted to modern high pressure pipeline technology.

In 1757 a high bridge, the Gosauzwang (see Walk Two) was constructed to carry the Soleleitungsweg a dizzy and dramatic 48 metres above the Gosau valley, a tributary from the Halstättersee, and though the present bridge is modern, it still makes a magnificent viewpoint.

One early method for producing the salt brine was for the miners to dig a pit in the rocks where there were salt levels and flood it with fresh water till the water loosened the salt. The salt then sank to the bottom of the pit and the resulting brine could then be pumped to the refinery.

At Ebensee where the pipeline ended, there was a prototype

of the first salt refinery. A giant vat made out of hammered sheet iron was placed above an enormous wood fire. Smoke and steam rose to the building's towering chimneyless roof and the salt was taken out when it reached a certain concentration and taken away to be dried - to produce the familiar refined white salt of the table. Brown coal was later used instead of wood for fires. A modern 'high-tech' refinery and chemical works at Ebensee now deals with a variety of saline-based products and continues a tradition of four hundred years of industrial development in the region.

But until the building of the railway and the improvement of the road in the later 19th century, the Salzkammergut was effectively sealed off geographically from the outside world. It was comparatively easy therefore for the Salt Office (Salzamt) to forbid anyone from outside the area to enter this domain unless a special pass had been obtained. The aim was to avoid the smuggling of untaxed salt, because the lucrative salt trade helped to swell the Emperor's coffers and salt increasingly became a government monopoly. Regulations were made to supply the salt centres with provisions from the surrounding areas, with severe penalties attached in case of default. The government for a long time regulated which harbours could be used for the salt trade and which markets should be supplied with provisions at fixed prices. Up to the present day, anyone in the Salzkammergut who is in the throes of presenting a virtually hopeless case to the authorities, is cynically told to 'take it to the Salt Office' (which of course no longer exists in its old form) for clearance.

In conjunction with salt production, forestry too was an important industry in the region because wood was needed for various salt refining processes, for the wooden support walls in the tunnels and galleries and of course, for boat building. The forests were also a huntsman's paradise with roe and fallow deer, chamois and wild boar.

It had originally been discovered that brine baths or 'Sole' was effective in treating the salt miners for rheumatism and skin complaints and the salt springs later came to be used for a number of gynaecological and infant diseases while the sulphur springs of Bad Ischl and Bad Goisern (as they came to be known - 'Bad' means bath) proved effective for curing or at least improving various ailments connected with joints, muscles, nervous system and for various skin troubles. Bath and mud treatment were found to be useful in soothing inflammation of the joints, and iodised springs could help metabolic and circulation disorders and vision and glandular troubles.

Today the Austrian Saltworks Company - Österreische Salinen AG - produces 700,000 m³ of industrial brine annually and 400,000 tons of salt from its mines in Salzkammergut and Land Salzburg. Only 7% of the salt is actually used as table salt because as well as being a necessary trace element in the human diet, it is very useful in numerous manufacturing processes. Ironically the salt mines which were once the source of so much treasure, became repositories during the last war of treasure of a different kind - the hiding places of works of art of international importance, a place of safety from the ravages of war.

During a visit to the Bad Ischl, Hallstatt or Bad Aussee Salt Mines, suitably clad in your borrowed overalls, riding on an old mine railway truck deep into the mine, and sliding down a long wooden shoot to a spectacularly lit brine lake before returning above ground to the entrance tunnel with its ancient symbol of crossed hammers, you are close to nearly three thousand years of human history and endeavour. Well may the miners' traditional greeting of 'Gluck auf!' ('Good luck!') ring in your ears.

BAD ISCHL - AN EMPEROR'S RESORT

In 1848, eighteen year old Emperor Franz Joseph I, the penultimate Habsburg monarch, ascended the throne at a time of turmoil in European politics. Austria at this time was master of a huge empire incorporating Czechs, Serbs, Hungarians, Slavs and many other peoples, all of them straining at the leash for a measure of independence. Franz Joseph's uncle had already been forced to abdicate as too moderate and too ready to grant demands which had some leaning towards democracy. Young Franz Joseph saw himself as destined to breathe life into the ancient Habsburg empire and return it to its former glory, reminiscent of the 18th century splendours of the Empress Maria Theresa and her son Emperor Josef II.

There are interesting parallels and differences between Franz Joseph and King Ludwig II of Bavaria, 'the Dream Prince' (see *The King Ludwig Way* by the present authors, uniform with this volume) who also ascended the throne aged eighteen in 1864 as a golden youth, but whose reign ended tragically in forced abdication and early death in highly suspicious circumstances. His cousin, the Empress Elisabeth of Austria, one of the few people with a real understanding of this strange, complex individual, was left to mourn him, movingly, by laying a simple wreath of jasmine on his coffin. Her own husband, Franz Joseph, far less glamorous and with none of Ludwig's cultural sensitivity, proved much more tenacious as a monarch and ruled for 68 years - longer than Queen Victoria - till his death at the age of 86.

The little Alpine resort of Bad Ischl had a close and deep involvement with the Emperor Franz Joseph's life. Not only did he spend 83 of his 86 summers there, but a number of momentous personal and political events took place in the town. Ischl or Isch(a)la under the Celts had, like Hallstatt, long been involved with the salt trade and was also noted for its brine baths, before developing in the 19th century as a typical small inland health spa where people came to drink the mineral water from local springs in the elegant 'Trinkhalle' or immerse themselves in salty waters.

Franz Joseph's mother, Princess Sophie, after two years of childlessness, had taken the advice of her Viennese doctor, Dr. Wirer, and tried the Ischl brine baths. Within two years her first son was born - 'The Salt Prince' - and she was later to become the mother of two more sons. The fame of the Ischl cure spread. Bad Ischl soon became the centre of a highly sophisticated and aristocratic circle and the young Prince, later Emperor, regularly returned to Ischl every year for his birthday celebrations in August, and soon began to enjoy a passion for hunting in the surrounding forests. The future of the resort was assured.

The Bavarian Princess Helene, the young Emperor's cousin, was originally chosen as a suitable royal consort, and she, her mother and younger sister were invited to Ischl to meet the Emperor. He, however, fell deeply in love with her younger sixteen year old sister Elisabeth (Sissi) and their engagement was speedily announced at the Hotel Austria in Ischl in 1853. This same building by the River Traun, with its triple gables and with Rococo-style facade was previously known as the See-auer House and had belonged to a wealthy salt refiner who was allowed to store the salt before shipment down river. It is now the town's art gallery and museum.

The Eltzvilla, at the foot of the Jainzenberg, was renovated and renamed the Kaiservilla and an elegant parkland laid out around it before being presented to the young couple as a wedding present by Princess Sophie. In the follow year Franz Joseph had the Marmorschlößl built in the grounds for the Empress, which became a favourite retreat where she read and composed poetry. Today the Marmorschlößl has become a well laid out museum of photography and the Kaiservilla with its 50,000 hunting trophies, carefully labelled, are a witness to the Emperor's passion for the sport - he was an excellent shot. Both these villas and the grounds make an interesting half-day outing in Ischl itself - easily combined with Walk Three and Four.

Within a few years, the Empress Elisabeth found the stifling rigidity of Viennese court life alien to her temperament and took refuge in numerous journeys abroad. It was sad that such a beautiful and gifted woman with modern ideas on exercise, a strenuous walker and superb horsewoman who followed a daily programme of gymnastics, became increasingly obsessed with her figure and appearance, indulging in strange near-starvation diets. She became increasingly alienated from her husband.

The marriage experienced its share of tragedy when in 1889 at Mayerling, a hunting lodge not far from Vienna, Crown Prince Rudolf, their only son, took his own life and that of his young mistress, Marie Vetsera. This caused a great scandal which clumsy attempts to deflect by hurrying Marie's body away in secret to Heiligenkreuz for burial, did nothing to

avert. The heir to the throne had requested papal annulment of
an unhappy marriage in order to be free to marry Marie, and a
furious quarrel with his father seemingly led to this suicide
pact. You pass the plaque erected by a proud father to
commemorate Prince Rudolph's first shooting of a deer in
1867 in the forest in Jainzental, on Walk Four - an area where
the Empress herself often exercised.

Contrary to popular belief, the death of their son failed to
bring Emperor and Empress together though in 1867 Elisabeth
had worked hard to promote the Hungarian cause, the country
being dear to her heart. She is credited with helping to bring
about the Dual Monarchy of Austria-Hungary, so that Franz
Joseph also became King of Hungary; a state of affairs which
lasted nearly 50 years.

Ischl increasingly became not just the Emperor's favourite
summer holiday area and hunting region, but also a place
where visiting heads of state could be seen in a relatively
relaxed atmosphere under the guise of attendance at the
Kaiser's birthday celebrations. Britain's King Edward VII
came to Ischl in 1905, 1906 and 1908, hoping to influence the
Emperor to curb Germany's growing power and isolate her
politically - but without success. In 1908 Austria occupied
Bosnia and Herzegovina and the Balkan territories became
increasingly a thorn in the imperial flesh, culminating in the
notorious events of 1914 when the Kaiser, now in his 80s and
in poor health, went on holiday to Ischl earlier than usual. His
nephew and heir, the Archduke Ferdinand, insisted against
the Emperor's advice on going to review the manoeuvres in
Bosnia with his wife. A Serbian assassin's bullet struck them
down at Sarajevo and with this provocation came a more or less
inevitable chain of events. Some claim that the Habsburgs
were waiting for an excuse to clip Serbia's wings as it had
become a rallying point for Slav disaffection within the
Austrian empire. From the Kaiservilla in Ischl an Ultimatum
was sent to Serbia for the outrage. The Kaiser's desk and the
fateful transcript can still be seen there. The wording was such
as to make certain terms unacceptable and the Serbian reply
made mobilisation inevitable.

It is incredible to believe that in the beautiful, peaceful surroundings of Bad Ischl, a few pen strokes at an unassuming desk in the Kaiservilla set in train the momentous and tragic events of the First World War which changed the face of Europe and indeed the world and cost millions of lives.

Soon after that the Emperor left Ischl for the last time for Vienna, and his own death followed in two years and with it the end of an era. The Empress Elisabeth had herself been murdered in 1898 in Geneva by an anarchist and a small room in the Kaiservilla where she wrote her letters has appropriate memorabilia.

Ischl had been dear to the Kaiser also for its associations with a very close friend, the actress Katherina Schratt who became the Emperor's confidant. A secret path led between the Kaiservilla and the Villa Felicitas, her holiday residence, so that the Kaiser might breakfast with her privately. His letters to her are in rather more relaxed vein than those to his wife and were obviously necessary to this strange, lonely, rather pedantic man who rose daily about 4.00 or 5.00am and did all his paperwork methodically with an immense sense of duty. It is impossible to compare the comparatively spartan Kaiservilla with the splendour of Ludwig II's of Bavaria's various palaces - the Kaiservilla was essentially a hunting lodge. However, in both the Kaiservilla and the Emperor's Royal Palace, the Hofburg, in Vienna, a simple iron bedstead was the Emperor's preference in his sleeping quarters, as he felt that he wanted to identify with his own soldiers. Paradoxically, he rigidly insisted on enormous punctilio; the story goes that when in old age he was suffering one night from severe breathing difficulties, he sent his hurriedly roused doctor home again to dress more correctly in formal 'tails' before he would see him.

The Emperor was frequently seen in military uniform or, at Ischl, in traditional hunting costume - a grey-green jacket, tufted hat and lederhosen. The actual costume he wore is on display in the Kaiservilla and has been carved in over-life-sized detail on his imposing statue deep in the forest near Ischl, the Kaiser Jagdstandbild, in the nearby woods, erected on the Emperor's 80th birthday (see Walk Three). It is to misunderstand his personality to believe that this ethnic hunting dress was an attempt to be nearer his people, though that is what his people fondly believed and wanted to believe. Up to this very day a Kaisermesse (Emperor's Mass), is performed on the anniversary of his birthday in the Bad Ischl parish church and is always heavily over-subscribed.

His long reign, personal misfortunes and idiocyncracies and great sense of duty caused him to be seen retrospectively as a great father figure, rather than a deeply conservative monarch whose time, politically, was running out. As a member of the Habsburg dynasty, he gave Austria a sense of identity in her chequered history of invasion, shifting frontiers and polyglot racial mix. He and the Empress Elisabeth came to represent a symbol of a more glamorous and romantic past when Austria was still a world power in a rather less frightening and less complicated world. The Kaiser's death in 1916 meant that he never became associated with the imminent disintegration of the Austro-Hungarian Empire.

But Ischl has also other memories and other glories. It became a centre for the arts, most particularly music. Composers also came to be inspired both by the beauty of the lakes and mountains and by the sophisticated and fashionable Viennese who came in their hundreds on the direct express trains from the capital to Attnang-Pucheim before catching the little branch line train along the Salzkammergut railway to join their Emperor at his summer resort.

Anton Bruckner, composer of mighty symphonies, frequently played on the Ischl parish church organ whilst staying with his friend in a villa alongside the River Traun. Johannes Brahms, who stayed in both Bad Ischl (where Gustav Mahler came to see him) and Altaussee, composed many works whilst staying in the area.

But it was the more light hearted world of Viennese operetta that soon came to have a particular association with Ischl. Such legendary masters of the Viennese operetta stage as waltz-king Johann Strauss, (you can still eat at the Café Ramsauer, one of Strauss's favourite haunts in Ischl), Friedrich Kalman, Oscar Strauss and many others spent a good deal of their time during the summer months at Ischl.

It was also here in Ischl that Franz Lehar bought his villa by the River Traun, which you can visit as a museum, (the 'Leharvilla'). In Bad Ischl he composed not only one of the most popular and melodically delightful musicals of all time - the 'Merry Widow' - but about two dozen other highly successfull operettas including 'Land of Smiles', 'Gypsy Love' and 'Frederike'. His villa is filled with his personal effects and many of the splendid gifts he received world-wide as a tribute to his music.

Bad Ischl also attracted singers, actors and opera stars of international reputation like Richard Tauber, Maria Jeritza and Alfred Piccaver, playwrights like Johann Nestroy and the acclaimed regional writer Adelbert Stifter who all came to Ischl to perform for its artistic clientele or to be inspired by the Salzkammergut scenery. Artists like Altdorfer, the brothers von Alt, Gauermann and Makart also discovered the Salzkammergut and have left us their inimitable response to the area.

Nowadays you can still drink the waters in the Biedermeier-style Trinkhalle and listen to some delightful concerts of classical music. (Biedermeier is the name of the 19th century decorative style which is a kind of lighter and more middle class and comfortable version of the 18th century baroque. It was used for the facades of many villas in Ischl and Gmunden.) Between July and early September each year there is a summer repertoire of a Lehar operetta and one by another composer at the Kurhaus, where it is possible to mingle with an audience, many of whom are dressed in exquisitely beautiful evening dirndls (traditional Austrian costume) in sumptuous fabrics, to enjoy an interval drink of sparkling wine and to lose oneself in the bitter-sweet melodies, charm and gaiety of an operetta's magical world of romantic fantasy.

Nowhere sums up Bad Ischl's aura of far-from-faded elegance better than Zauner's Konditorei, which once provided the imperial court with cakes and pastries, though to English ears the words 'cake' or 'pastry' are totally inappropriate, failing to convey the variety and sophistication of such exquis-

ite confections, beautifully served with a small glass of water to
clear the palate. Whether you like a feather-light sponge with
whipped cream and wild strawberries, or a Torte subtly flavoured, this is an experience to relish. The original Zauner's on
Pfarrgasse is open during normal shop hours, but a more
recently opened branch which includes a restaurant is charm-
ingly situated by the River Traun and is open till late into the
evening.

But Bad Ischl is still renowned as a spa with its health-giving
waters and mud baths. The modern Kurmittelhaus is one of
the best equipped in Austria and has an underground passage
linking it directly with the Kurhotel where all kinds of steam,
sauna, brine and inhalation treatments are available. It was
discovered in the early nineteenth century that since the salt
mine brine had a much higher average salt concentration, at
27%, than the sea which averaged 3.5% (the Dead Sea has
24%), it followed that the curative powers of sea bathing for
certain illnesses would be even more enhanced by brine baths.
In 1821 Dr. Wirer with a number of colleagues opened the
Ischl brine baths which had to be expanded four years later.
The birth of 'The Salt Prince' and the coming of the railway
accelerated the rise of Bad Ischl as a spa till by the end of the
century, the numbers of visitors had increased five-fold.

Taking the waters or 'the Cure' is not just simply a matter of
medical treatment, it is part of a whole ambiance of strolling
round the Kurpark listening to the orchestra, or to a concert in
the Trinkhalle, enjoying the facilities of the Kurhaus and
sauntering round elegant small shops on the Traun promenade
and making excursions - by train, postbus or car - into a
compellingly beautiful hinterland of lakeland and mountain
scenery. For rambler as much as Emperor, it is difficult to
imagine a more convenient or delightfully located setting.

PRACTICAL POINTS
Accommodation and Travel
Salzkammergut has a huge range of accommodation available
to visitors from five star hotels to youth hostel, farmhouse and
self catering, most of it at prices which are notably cheaper

than the UK when quality and price are compared. In particular it is possible to get bed and breakfast accommodation in a Pension or in a 'Privatzimmer' (private house) even in the peak season at rates which start from as little as 90-100ös (less than £5) per day for bed and breakfast for a room without facilities - though you'll pay more for full facilities and a central location. A typical 'Hotel Garni' with en suite facilities costs around £10-£12 per person per night, high season - of a quality which would usually cost around 50% more in Britain.

Bad Ischl is undoubtedly the best location for anyone wanting to explore the region without a car, situated as it is at a nodal point of the transport network in terms of train services and bus services, which in typical Austrian fashion, always leave the station forecourt. Gmunden and Bad Aussee whilst being excellent centres in their own right are both some distance from their main railway station, though the former has a shuttle tram service from the town centre and the latter has Postbuses which meet all the main trains. St. Wolfgang, though it has an excellent choice of accommodation, is a good 35-40 minutes away from Bad Ischl by bus for connecting buses and trains which adds to the cost and time of travel.

For anyone arriving by air at Salzburg Airport, Bad Ischl can be reached by direct express Postbus from Salzburg Railway Station (Service 3000 - last bus around 19.15). If you fly to either Munich or Vienna there are direct express train services to Attnang-Pucheim Station between Salzburg and Linz for the local train service on the Salzkammergutbahn to Gmunden, Bad Ischl and Bad Aussee.

Rail is an extremely good way of travelling to Austria, using one of the overnight ferries (Harwich-Hook being the most convenient, with connections via Köln, München and Salzburg through the Rhine valley on comfortable German Inter-City trains with excellent travelling restaurants, which can be a holiday in itself. Rail Travel is a particularly economic proposition if you hold one of the many railcards such as the Inter-Rail Card (under 26), a Senior Citizens Europe Card giving half-price travel in Europe and the newer Family Europe Railcard which allows any three or more people from the same household irrespective of age to travel for the price of one adult fare and two or more half-fares. These rail cards have the additional bonus of being valid on train services within Austria giving worthwhile reductions on local train services. Information about these European Rail Travel facilities can be obtained from BR Travel Centres.

If you are planning to use rail services a good deal within Austria itself, it is worthwhile knowing about bargain priced 'Landnetzkarte' or local Rail Rover tickets available for 9 or 16 days and valid on both öBB and private lines within the Salzkammergut region, as well Wolfgangsee Lake Steamers. They can be bought on the first day of travel at local stations. A free leaflet (available in English) from main stations will explain these and various additional bargain rail fares available for travellers.

Otherwise, you'll find that bus and rail fares are broadly similar to the UK with Day Return fares available on most of the return trips suggested in this book.

The complete timetable of the Salzkammergut Railway is in Thomas Cook's European Timetable available in the UK at any Thomas Cook's Branch, but utterly invaluable is the pocket-sized Austrian National Railways Kursbuch or Fahrpläne, issued each May, costing 100ös (around £5) which contains full details of all öBB (State Railway) train and boat services, plus private and local railways, city tramways and busways, boat services on all the Salzkammergut lakes and cable-car services. The Salzkammergut Railway Line on which most of the walks in this book are based is Table 17 in the Austrian Kursbuch. One useful point is that with the exception of early morning commuter or workers' trains, the Sunday train service is broadly the same as weekdays. Bus services do differ more, with some additional buses on tourist routes on Sundays.

Missing are the öBB's bus services (of limited value to walkers in the Salzkammergut) and the yellow Postbuses. Details of the postbuses are available in a booklet Postbus Fahrpläne - Salzkammergut which is available free of charge from local Post Offices. The timetable is revised at the end of

May each year at the same time as the rail timetable to ensure connections are kept.

Look out for the little crossed hammer symbol on both bus and rail timetables signifying weekdays only on bus and train times, and the cross ($\dagger$) symbol indicating services that only run on Sundays or public holidays.

Initial contact for accommodation and information about the region (state which town/resorts preferred) is The Regional Tourist Office, Salzkammergut-Verkehrverband A1-4820 Bad Ischl, Kreuzplatz 23, AUSTRIA. Tel: (from UK) 010 43 6132 6909.

Austria Travel Ltd. is the Anglo-Austrian Society's own travel agency (Atol 065) - but it is more than just another agency. With staff in London and in Vienna, the Society's expertise and experience over the past 40 years provides Austrian holidays of quality for the discerning traveller. Austria Travel respects individual wishes and takes care of all travel needs - flights, hotels, transfers, car hire and insurance. They can also offer reduced rate rail bookings from anywhere in the UK to Gatwick or Heathrow. Austria Travel currently offers hotels in Salzburg, Gmunden, Bad Ischl, Bad Aussee, along with highly competitive rates to other resorts throughout Austria, and best rates for flights to Vienna, Salzburg, Klagenfurt and Graz. They can be contacted at 46 Queen Anne's Gate, Westminster, London, SW1H 9AU. Tel: 01 222 0366 or 01 222 2430.

The Leeds-based Pennine-Euro Travel of 6-10 Green Road, Meanwood, Leeds, LS6 4JP. Tel: 0532 785597 specialises in both air and rail travel from anywhere in the UK to the Continent and can also book through travel and accommodation for walkers using this book.

Both these agencies know Austria well and are likely to give much more detailed information about services to the Salzkammergut than most high street travel agency chains who handle mainly package tour bookings to the most popular (from the UK) holiday destinations.

Information about Austria is also available from the Austrian National Tourist Office, 30 St. George Street, London, W1R

0AL. Tel: 01 629 0461.

Climate, Clothing and Rights of Way

The climate of Upper Austria is more extreme than the United
Kingdom. Winters are colder with heavy snowfalls, making
the region excellent for traditional skiing or for cross-country
skiing, and the summer is hotter but, like any lake or mountain
area, subject to dramatic changes and sudden heavy storms.
Though July and August average temperature can get well into
the upper 20°s to lower 30°s Centigrade (80°s-90°s Fahren-
heit) you can, even at that time of the year, get periods of cloud
and rain with midday temperatures down to 10° or less - deci-
dedly cool. Such fluctuations even over a period of two or three
days dictate a wide choice of clothes from light summer shirts
and shorts to windproof jackets and woollies and, of course,
British-type rainwear capable of keeping out Lake District-
style vertical rain - though such downpours don't usually last
long and the British pattern of endless days of grey clouds and
fine drizzle are mercifully rare. Weather is more reliable early
and late in the season, and September and even October offers
cool, clear days, ideal for walking and superb colours, though
nights can be cool. So whatever time of the year you come, a
fairly wide range of clothes will have to find their way into suit-
case or rucksack.

Remember though, that later in the season many attractions
are closed and public transport services less comprehensive.
You may have to modify plans and even use the occasional taxi
to fill in gaps after late September and before late May.

Some of these walks are perfectly possible in stout shoes or
even trainers if the weather is good, but a lightweight pair of
boots is recommended for comfort on all but the shortest of
walks. Always carry rainwear (blue skies can turn to thunder-
storms in the Alps in a matter of minutes), some emergency
food and a decent map in a light rucksack. Insect repellant is
strongly recommended in the summer months as the forests do
breed both midges and horseflies that can cause swollen joints
if they attack a sensitive spot, plus a suitable antiseptic cream if
the creatures do penetrate the repellant. A first aid pack will

save possible expensive chemists' bills - it goes without saying that you will have taken out insurance to cover medical and other accidental expenses. Austria, at time of writing, is not yet within the EEC and member states' reciprocal medical insurances (the familiar Form E111) does not apply.

Though local walking maps exist in a confusing variety, don't expect to find anything to match the superb accuracy and clarity of the Ordnance Survey 1:25,000 'Pathfinder' Series or even the 1:50,000 'Landranger' Series. Probably most useful and reliable for your needs are the 1:50,000 Kompass Wanderkarte (sheets 18, 19, 20) or the Freytag and Berndt sheets WK 281,282 at the same scale, available at most local bookshops and tourist offices in the area, or Stanfords, 12/14 Long Acre, London, WC2E 9LP. The appropriate maps are listed in each walk. From our experience neither are 100% reliable, and indeed depend on users for updated information. Nor can you always depend on waymarking which varies from the excellent to the non-existent (in spite of what the maps indicate). As in the UK, waymarking is largely a voluntary activity undertaken by one of the Alpine or Naturfreunde clubs, (usual colours red, white and red or sometimes just red) with local tourist associations often undertaking excellent work in their locality with good clear footpath signs at key points, though in a variety of colours and styles. By using map, book and waymarks in conjunction hopefully you'll experience no problems.

Unlike the UK where access is often difficult even in popular tourist areas, there is a presumption of access along a road, track or footpath in Austria unless access is physically barred (unusual) or deterred by such notices as 'Eintritt Verboten' or 'Privatweg' on a private drive. Miles of forest road ('Forstweg') are open to the public. Most alpine meadows are unenclosed, but as in upland Britain it is only courtesy to keep to paths across working farmland to reduce disturbance and trampling to an absolute minimum and to avoid disturbing privacy. Wild flowers are legally protected, and it goes without saying that readers of this book leave no litter and guard against the risk of fires in forestry areas - including carelessly discarded matches or cigarettes.

Food

Food is one of the many delights of a holiday in Austria, both as regards quality, service, variety and chance to try out particular specialities. Austria's former empire with its mixture of races and actual geographical position have influenced the cuisine and enriched it while the addition of more delicate spices and flavourings, have produced inimitable versions of Balkan or Moravian dishes.

Breakfast (Frühstück) consists generally of excellent freshly ground coffee, though tea is always available. Coffee is one of the relics of the Turkish sieges - the Turks after besieging Vienna, allegedly fled leaving their sacks of coffee behind to the delight of the inhabitants.

Tea, however, is drunk as a far weaker blend than is usual in England as it is normally drunk either with lemon or 'schwarz' literally black, meaning without milk or lemon. Whilst you can have milk in your tea English-style, it is often too weak for the English palate and unless two teabags are used, it tastes better without. Milk is plentiful and it is often offered hot with your breakfast coffee.

Several varieties of bread are readily obtainable in shops or restaurants, including rye bread and a variety of rolls, especially *Kaiser Semmel,* a type of round roll with 4 deeply etched quarters on top, this very characteristic shape is quite a triumph of the baker's art as the original pieces of dough start as a square. A selection of thinly sliced local cheeses such as the locally produced Schardinger or Traunsee cheese (also excellent in a toasted sandwich with ham for a quick lunch snack - *Schinken-Käsetoast),* cold meats which tend to be the more delicately flavoured Wursts or sausages though salami is here a better term, including ham which is much less salty than our own English version and nicely flavoured, eggs usually boiled (the Austrians are particularly fond of very lightly boiled eggs so specify if you prefer them harder) and some splendid preserves or honey rather than marmalade or jam complete the meal.

Lunch time (Mittagessen) is often the main meal of the day, but there is no problem if a snack, sandwich or light lunch is preferred when you are out walking and the main meal can just as easily be taken in the evening (Abendessen).

If you decide to make sandwiches or carry a snack with you for lunch, local supermarkets invariably have an excellent choice of rolls, cooked meats, biscuits, fruit, canned drinks at prices which are broadly similar to the UK, and probably with a wider choice, especially if you are prepared to branch out and try things not normally available at home. Quality is invariably high.

Best value if you are eating out for lunch or dinner is the 'Tagesmenu' that most restaurants offer, a table d'hote at a fixed price consisting of three courses and there is sometimes even a choice here of more than one fixed menu. Prices start at about 60-70ös - around £3.50, and average around 100ös - around £5 - notably cheaper than the UK.

Soups can be the more substantial and meaty *Gulaschsuppe*, or *Leberknödelsuppe*, a soup with a large dumpling flavoured with finely chopped liver - all most welcome on cold days or after a fair amount of exercise. Clear soups with pasta, *Nudelsuppe;* or with finely chopped pancakes, *Fritattensuppe;* vegetable soups, *Gemusesuppe;* pea soup, *Erbsensuppe;* are all a good start to a meal and particularly recommended when available is *Knoblauchsuppe,* a cream of garlic soup made with typical Austrian finesse.

Fresh fish from the many Salzkammergut lakes and rivers is a joy whether it be trout *(Forelle), Reinanke,* a trout-like fish only found in the area and the pink-fleshed *Saibling* or char in English which can be accompanied with the merest hint of creamed horseradish and cranberries. Fish can often be marked on the menu as costing according to weight 'pro dg' in other words by decca gramm, but is very good value.

Meat dishes are varied from the Hungarian inspired *Gulasch* flavoured with paprika to the famous *Wiener Schnitzel* and many more. This is an escalope of veal *(Kalb)* or *(Schwein)* pork, fried in egg and breadcrumbs and usually served with a salad and parsley sprinkled potatoes. Other Schnitzel are *Pariser Art* without the breadcrumbs; with sour cream, *Rahmschnitzel* or *Zigeuner Art* with onions and peppers. *Zwiebelrost-*

braten is a delicious portion of roast beef in a rich onion gravy while beef steaks, medallions of veal or pork are also available should you be feeling less adventurous. *Tafelspitz* is a lean cut of boiled beef served with vegetables in a chive flavoured sauce. *Cevapcci* or *Fleischlaibchen* are delicious meat rissoles served again with vegetables or salad. Chicken such as *Brathuhn* (fried chicken) and Turkey escalopes (*Indian* or *Truthahn)* are also popular. Venison dishes are a particular delight of the region such as *Rehbraten, Gemsebraten* and *Hirschbraten* usually served with *Knödeln,* the Austrian dumplings which are very light, delicately flavoured and usually based on a breadcrumb mixture. A variety of salads or vegetables accompany the main dishes and rice *(Reis)* and pasta *(Nudeln)* are just as likely to be offered as potatoes *(Kartoffeln)* for your main course.

The standard term for dessert is *Nachtisch* and you then have the difficult job of deciding between a number of equally tempting gateaux, puddings and ices. There is often a separate ice-cream menu with a number of imaginative variations on the ice theme, but if you would like something particularly refreshing, do try *Eiskaffee,* a tall glass of ice cold coffee with ice-cream, topped by whipped cream and served with both spoon and straw. Hot desserts are known generically as *Mehlspeisen* as they generally contain *Mehl* (flour). A great speciality is *Salzburgernockerln,* a souffle light as air which is ample for 2 to 3 people and should be served with a slightly sharp-tasting fruit compote. *Palatschinken,* the Austrian pancake, has a variety of possible fillings including fruit and *Topfen* (the light creamy cottage cheese similar to German Quark). *Kaiserschmarren* is a further variation on the pancake theme with a rather charming story. The name *Schmarren* really means something of little value, rather a contradiction in terms. The story goes that Kaiser Franz Joseph I stopped at a Gasthaus for refreshment while out hunting and the maidservant over-awed at the visit managed to break the pancakes she was making for the dessert. Her mistress helped her to make a feature of this mishap, and they were served with a dusting of sugar after being torn with two forks and served with a fruit compote to the Emperor's

35

evident satisfaction. He enquired the name of the dish and was told *Kaiserschmarren*. *Apfelstrudel*, the famous Austrian speciality, actually had its origins in Turkey, its paperthin pastry is rolled over layers of apples, raisins and cinnamon and can be served with a helping of whipped cream. Popular variations of the strudel theme are *Topfenstrudel* with raisins and Austrian cottage cheese filling, or other fruits such as grapes or cherries.

Austria is the land of excellent cakes, and the litany of *Torten* would need a whole chapter to itself, but mention must be made of the famous *Sacher Torte* which is a dark chocolate cake layered with apricot comfiture and with a dark chocolate glaze; a helping of whipped cream being optional. One of the best Sachertorten we have ever eaten was high up in the Salzkammergut in a little mountain Alm. *Malakofftorte* is a Torte made of layers of delicate sponge fingers in a finely flavoured cream, *Punschtorte* as its name implies is flavoured with alcohol and has a characteristic pink icing, while *Topfentorte* can be either baked in the oven or made as a cheesecake with a setting agent. *Obstorte* has fruits of the season on a rich sponge base cut into squares, while other confections of nuts, chocolate and pastry can be enjoyed in turn. If you prefer a plainer style cake, then the *Guglhupf* in a characteristic tall ring shape is an excellent accompaniment to a cup of coffee.

There is a local tax on all drinks in Austria taken in any place of refreshment, which makes them noticeably dearer than in Britain, but the money raised is used to help maintain local amenities such as footpaths and signposts. You are also able to sit as long as you like sipping your chosen beverage without, as happens in England, feeling obliged to buy another drink or move on. Beer is of good quality and German in style. Wine, though the Salzkammergut does not produce its own wine, is normally white and on the dry side and is also a good buy whether it be Grüner Vetliner or Riesling-Sylvaner type. There are a few excellent red wines available like Blauer Portugaiser and Blaufrankisch.

Austrian cider, *Most*, is also locally produced and is dry and strong like the scrumpies of England's West Country and much enjoyed in this area. At the end of the day a schnapps or strong liqueurs like *Obstler* (fruit based) and *Enzian* (Gentian) are another Austrian speciality, (to be drunk in a single gulp) but if you prefer a sweeter flavour, there is a very fine Apricot or *Marillen* liqueur. There is a wide variety of non-alcoholic drinks available from *Apfelsaft* (apple juice), *Orangensaft*, (orange juice) other fruits like *Traubensaft* (grape juice) to various proprietary brands such as Cappy. Almdoodler is a mixture of wine and lemonade without alcohol content. Mineral water *(Mineralwasser)*, of which there are many brands from local health-springs, are all good, and there is the ubiquitous Coco Cola or Fanta (orangeade).

Coffee and cakes can be taken as a snack or light lunch any time of day as can a roll with Frankfurter or Wurst (a salami-style sausage), and if you see the sign *Bretteljause*, this indicates that a traditional platter of cold meats, peasant cheese and black bread are served, forming either a light lunch, evening meal or late afternoon snack. A local speciality in Salzkammergut is *Topfenbrot* which consists of bread and *Liptauer*, a delicious cream cheese delicately flavoured with paprika.

Marialm

Soleleitungsweg near Ebensee

PART TWO - THE SALZKAMMERGUT WAY

WALK ONE: KOPPENBRÜLLER HOHLE - HALLSTATT - 10km (6 miles) Easy

Starting Point: Obertraun Koppenbrüller Station (öBB). This rail halt is closed from the end of September until the beginning of May, when the caves are closed. Outside this period use Obertraun Station - 3km by road or parallel high level footpath (Obertraun Höhenweg).

Finishing Point: Hallstatt Station (no road access).

Motorists: Park near Koppenrast Guest-house and return by train.

Refreshments: Gasthaus Koppenrast (100m from station); Dachsteinhof, Haus am See Obertraun; Hallstatt Station (light refreshments only); Hallstatt town.

Major attractions: Koppenbrüller Cave; Dachstein Ice Caves and Mammoth Cave; Hallstatt.

Maps: Wanderkarte 20; F&B WK281

From the station platform and waiting room follow the main road right, across the bridge over the River Traun. Cross to the track which forms the entrance to the Koppenbrüller Hohle (cave) clearly signed. This track, about 1km long, ascends a deep narrow gorge shared only by the river and the railway which finally curves through a nature reserve into the cave entrance.

Remember to wear warmer clothing if you intend to visit the cave as cave temperature is normally about 6°C throughout the year. A feature of this cave and addition to the atmosphere are the shadows thrown by the flickering oil lamps handed out to the visitor as they wind their way round the cave complex. The name 'brüller' derives from 'brüllen', to roar; the underground waters of the Dachstein flow through the cave and the pounding water is an awe-inspiring sight to see and hear. Flooding at certain times from melting ice or excessive rain will cause the caves to be closed, but there is a highly efficient early

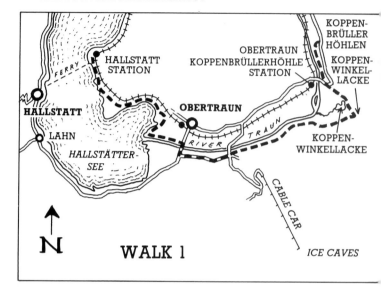

warning system.

Koppenbrüller Cave is open daily from May until the end of September - tours every hour, on the hour, last group at 16.00.

Return to the main road. Your route continues past the Gasthaus Koppenrast - an excellent coffee or even lunch stop - but soon after bear right along a stony track signed for the Koppenwinkelsee. You enter a nature reserve - semi-natural woodland under an awesome sheer cliff face. You pass a children's holiday home on the right, and enter deep woodland, the crags ever higher and, by the wayside, a massive boulder which fell off the face in February 1987 - a grim reminder of how unstable these cliffs can be.

But continue past the edge of Koppenwinkelacke, a small lake, deep in the forest which you can walk around - but otherwise keep ahead to Koppenwinkel Alm, a scatter of wooden barns and farm buildings, now used as simple holiday accommodation.

Your way is along a forest path immediately to the right

Obertraun, Hallstättersee

before the Alm, signed to Obertraun and (slightly faded) the Bundessportschule. The way begins as a broad path but soon narrows through dense woodland, its fringes rich in wild flowers including many kinds of orchids. Cross a series of wooden footbridges over fast flowing streams that hurtle down the mountainside. Keep ahead on the path, following the Obertraun signs, until it eventually reaches the riverside at a bridge.

Do not cross the bridge but keep alongside the river past a tiny memorial to a victim of a flood. Soon the wood thins to dense willow as the river, more sluggish, approaches Hallstättersee.

The path emerges at Dachsteinhof Restaurant - another place to quench hunger or thirst - and a crossroads. About 1km along the road to the left (signed) is the Dachsteinbahn - cabin lift - leading to the Ice Caves and Mammoth Caves (first stage), the summit of the Krippenstein (2.079m) (second stage) and the Dachstein Glacier (third stage).

A brief word of explanation regarding the prevalence of caves in the area may be of interest here. The limestone of the Dachstein range is affected by water that contains carbonic acid and the rock is also eroded by the activity of water itself. Rock movements throughout geological time have caused numberless cracks and crevices for the water to appear which trickles into the caves and becomes an underground drainage system. The Ice Cave - all year round ice is only rarely found - is a phenomenon of this kind. In winter the cold air sinks into the cave, cooling its walls like some natural refrigeration unit. When water appears, it freezes and hardly melts even in summer because the ice itself forms an additional cold storage system. The ice continues to increase, but although the caves themselves are thousands of years old, recents tests have shown that the ice is only about 500 years old. The names of the various caverns and passages have been taken from the sagas of Parsifal and the Holy Grail and the imaginative way these unique features of ice castles and towers have been lit, makes the experience into one of unforgettable enchantment.

The Mammoth Cave or Mammuthöhle is one of the biggest in Europe and its seemingly endless series of passages and halls are also dramatically lit and spotlight the activity of the water.

Both caves are open from May until the middle of October, but as the number of visitors to the Ice Caves are strictly limited each day for conservation reasons, visitors are advised to arrive early to book their place on a tour in advance.

To continue to Hallstatt, follow the minor road directly ahead from the crossroads which goes alongside the river, passing the Federal Sports School and the Youth Hostel. After just over a kilometre, at the next crossroads, turn right over the bridge towards Obertraun, but go first left immediately over the bridge along a track into the woods, signed with a handsome wooden sign 'Hallstättersee Ostufer Wanderweg'. The track soon narrows and bears right, over a footbridge - sharp left again here following the shoreline of the lake to a lido and Strandbad. The path goes behind these alongside a fence and emerges by the Haus am See, a hotel and restaurant. Keep ahead in front of the hotel where white arrows on the ground and sign will direct you left towards a jetty then right over a footbridge over a stream to the railway embankment.

The path is now easy to follow between railway and lakeside, with increasingly pretty views across the great bay which forms the southern end of the Hallstättersee. Keep left at a junction following the Lehrpfad - Nature Trail - signs. The trail has various typical trees and plants marked with their (German) names. Soon the path follows the railway inland, away from the shore, climbing steeply where the railway goes into a cutting, by an estate, eventually emerging at the lakeside again, with now quite superb views across the shimmering waters of the Hallstättersee with the little gleaming town of Hallstatt by the lake edge and below the mountainside.

The path emerges at the boat landing stage and railway station. Ferries cross the lake to Hallstatt town - a superb trip - and return to meet all trains. If you've time to fill before boat or train, the buffet in the station waiting room (up the steps) will supply refreshments. Alternatively you might like to continue along the Ostufer Wanderweg to Steeg Gosau - another superb walk - (see Walk 7 for the route in reverse direction). But Halstatt with its museums, market places, narrow streets, shops, two beautiful churches and salt mines will require more than one visit.

WALK TWO: HALLSTATT - BAD GOISERN - 15km (8 miles) Moderate

Starting Point: Hallstatt Town Centre - reached by boat from Hallstatt Station (öBB) or Postbus (2572) from Bad Ischl.

Finishing Point: Bad Goisern Station.

Motorists: Park at Bad Goisern Station and use the train. Hallstatt town congested and limited parking.

Refreshments: Hallstatt Town; Rudolfsturm (Hallstatt), Bad Goisern. Nothing directly on the central parts of the route from Rudolfsturm to Goisern, so take some refreshment with you.

Major attractions: Hallstatt, Prehistory and Folk Museum; Hallstatt Salt Mines.

Maps: Wanderkarte 18; F&B WK281

43

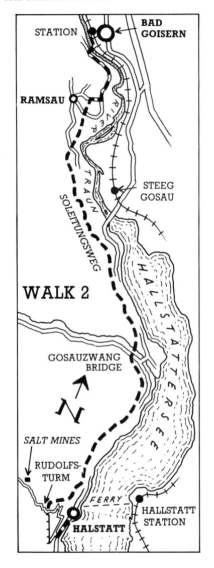

This walk can be very conveniently combined with a visit to Hallstatt with its exceptionally interesting museums and ancient salt mines. Time your visit to see these things in the morning and enjoy the afternoon's walk along the Soleleitungsweg - the world's oldest pipeline - to make a perfect day. The start of the Soleleitungsweg, down some steep steps and rugged steps around a cliff edge, whilst perfectly easy and safe might just induce vertigo in anyone without a head for heights. This is also a route subject to *Steinschlag* - rockfall - so be alert. An alternative route from Hallstatt is to follow the Ostufer Weg on the east shore from the station - see Walk 7.

From Hallstatt's market-place make your way to the top left-hand corner of the picturesque market-square, following the signs to the Prehistory and the 'Heimat' (Folk) Museum, past which a narrow lane, dedicated to the memory of Friederich Morton, the Hallstatt historian, goes through and behind the old town, rich in atmosphere. Look out, on the right, for a resting place where in former times women carrying those great baskets of rock salt paused to rest their aching backs.

The path emerges at Hallstatt Lahn, the newer, flatter side of the town which once contained the town's wharves where the salt and essential provisions were trans-shipped onto flat-bottomed boats. The familiar modern single nosed gondolas or 'Traunerl' on the Traunsee and Hallstättersee are descended from these boats.

Opposite the landing stage turn sharp right along a tarmac lane which leads to the funicular railway which ascends towards the salt mines and Rudolfsturm. You can avoid using the funicular by climbing the zig-zag path that ascends steeply behind the town - but the funicular, as well as being a little less hard on heart and lungs, is an experience in itself.

The track from the funicular leads up to the Halstatt salt mines; allow a good two hours if you decide to explore this remarkable complex of man-made caves and passages - one of the world's oldest salt mines in continuous use from prehistoric times to the present.

But the walk begins at Rudolfsturm, the remains of a castle built in 1284 by Rudolph of Habsburg, ruler of Austria, to

Avalanche shelter

protect the salt mines from his rivals, the Prince-archbishops in the Salzburg/Hallein area. It is now a restaurant.

Before leaving the tower (the last refreshment point before Bad Goisern) climb to the viewing terrace, immediately in front of and below the restaurant itself, for the breathtaking view of the Hallstättersee including an aerial view of Hallstatt itself, a brilliantly coloured crescent of roofs and housetops set against the incandescent blue of the lake; an image justifiably familiar on calendars and brochures throughout the world.

Take the path immediately below the Rudolfsturm signed 'Soleleitungsweg' and 'Goisern' which immediately descends steep wooden steps alongside a deep gorge down from the salt mines. Take care down here, particularly in wet weather. You cross a wooden footbridge and then join a narrow steep way almost chiselled out of the cliffside which follows an under-hang down the side of the gorge, down more steps, out into the main valley. You'll immediately notice the brine pipes - the oldest made of wood (many of which, discarded in heaps, you'll pass by the wayside), but most of iron. These pipelines follow you to the Ebensee, though the more modern versions still in use are made of concrete or high-grade plastic.

You now wind through tall woods, the Hallstättersee glimpsed between the trees, on a rocky shelf. This immensely beautiful path, numbered 601, forms part of the Northern Alpine Long Distance Route E4, a 3,500km route from Budapest to the Pyrenees - this being part of a strenuous loop over the summits of the limestone Alps.

You soon pass the entrance to one of the mine levels - Kaiser Franz Joseph Stoller, no longer used but with an imposing entrance, and the little cross hammer symbol over the arch.

As the path levels out this is easy walking, with constant superb views where the trees clear. At one point you must make your way under a waterfall where a little shelter protects you from water - and stones. A good 5 kilometres from the Rudolfsturm, the path descends by a fork - keep right - to cross a high iron bridge over a narrow pass at Gosau Mühle - the Gosauzwang - over the main road to Gosau. Keep ahead, again along a rocky shelf, but now losing height gradually, and dropping towards the road. About 1½km (1 mile) past the Gosau bridge, where the path has broadened to a forest track and begins to descend, take care not to miss the narrow path, which branches off left, with its red and white waymark on a tree, by a scree slope. This is the Soleleitungsweg.

Keep ahead now past the next junction (which takes you down to Steeg Gosau for buses and trains) down a narrower way, back into woodland. The route, well signed either as the Soleleitungsweg, the Soleweg or to Goisern, passes behind a hydro-electric works with its twin pipelines, the pylons unsightly but the power pollution free. You pass a hunting lodge, then the path leads behind an electro-plating works, descending to road level, through scattered woodland. At a junction turn left into a lane, but then go first right, signed Soleweg and Gschwandt, along a farmtrack by farms and freestanding houses.

At a crossroads go through a little pedestrian gate ahead, by houses (signed Nord Alpen Wanderweg) which now becomes an elevated path across a pleasant stretch of meadow. Bear right at the next junction along a gravel track, then left along a tarmac road - all waymarked. If this area is a little bit suburban, the houses are the Austrian variety whose balconies and window-boxes are a floral cornucopia - and beyond them lie vast panoramas of mountains, increasingly spectacular as the road ascends.

You cross a low summit. The road now descends towards the river. Keep ahead until you reach the bridge over the river, right. Cross. Bad Goisern town centre is straight ahead, but if you turn immediately left a wooded path goes between river and railway past Bad Goisern Station - the official path to the station is about 100 metres to the north beyond the goods yard, over a level crossing and bearing back right. A wooden cabin by the station has welcoming refreshment room tables inside or out from which to enjoy your drink and await your train.

WALK THREE: BAD GOISERN - BAD ISCHL - 13km (8 miles) Easy

Starting Point: Bad Goisern Station (öBB).

Finishing Point: Bad Ischl Station.

Motorists: Park at Bad Ischl or Bad Goisern and return by train.

Refreshments: Bad Goisern (Station), Gasthof Lauffen (closed Tuesdays); Bad Ischl (Station and in town).

Major attractions: Bad Goisern; Ischl town (see page 52); Katrin cable-car.

Maps: Wanderkarte 18; F&B WK281

Bad Goisern is a small spa town in the Traun Valley celebrated for its iodine and sulphur baths. There is a folk museum and a woodcutter's museum in the town. For those with the time and energy it's an excellent starting point for some fine hill walking, including the nearby Predigstuhl (1,276 metres) reached by the 'Ewige Wand' - the eternal wall - a path carved into the hillside.

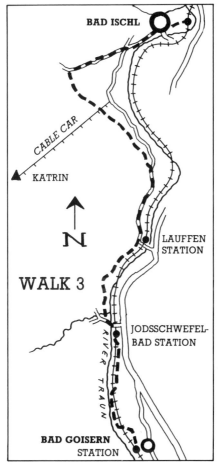

Come out of Bad Goisern Station along the station drive, but turn left by the telephone kiosk and Post Office, going alongside a fence by a small park. At the end of this track turn left again down a narrow path leading to the level crossing over the railway and the riverside path. Go right, down river, keeping on the same side of the river at the crossing bridge, along a

49

lovely section of riverside path known as the Traunreitersweg - named after the Traunriders - the men who between the 16th and the 19th century carried provisions by pack-pony along the banks of the Traun from its highest navigable point - the site of the Hotel Goldenes Schiff in Bad Ischl - to the Hallstättersee.

This riverside path continues by river and railway to Goisern Jodsschwefelbad Station. Keep ahead by a group of large timber garages to the river bridge. Cross here, passing a timber yard to the hamlet of Weißenbach (refreshments). The route now turns right immediately past the fire station - look for the Soleweg sign. Cross a concrete bridge by a small waterfall, then follow the track again to the right, behind the woodyard, towards the river, again following Soleweg signs between buildings. Bear left along a lane parallel to the river. At a fork the Soleweg bears left (look for a blue sign), climbing slightly, and becoming more recognisably the route of the pipeline once again, above a farm, by fir trees and then meeting the railway as it crosses the river.

Ahead is the village of Lauffen dominated by its little baroque church and watermill. A level crossing, protected by swing barriers that close when a train comes, leads to a narrow wooden footbridge across the river and a path by the race of the watermill (which as the two hammer symbol indicates belongs to the Saltworks) that climbs into the village centre.

Lauffen has an attractive main street and a Gasthof at the bottom of the village with liquid and other comfort for walkers. On a more spiritual level the church is also worth a visit. Dedicated to Mary in the Shadows, it dates from the 15th century when it was a pilgrim's church, rebuilt in the Austrian baroque-style in 1705.

Return to the path on the far side of the river either by the same route or the broader track to Lauffen Station. Follow the lane past the station, but at the 30km restriction sign look for the path signed Soleweg and Bad Ischl which runs through the woodland parallel to the road. Keep ahead at the little shrine and junction, still parallel to the road, signed to Katrinseilbahn, but the Saltway begins to leave the road, climbing above the lane along a rocky shelf through woods.

Lauffen

As the river swings back towards the path, you reach an impressive bronze statue, the Kaiserjagdstandbild between path and lane of Kaiser Franz Joseph I wearing his hunting clothes (the originals of which are to be seen in the Kaiservilla Museum) having just slain an equally impressive stag. This was erected in 1910 by the Austrian Hunters' Federation to commemorate the Kaiser's 80th birthday.

200 metres past the statue keep left past a pillar announcing the start of the Franz Carl Promenade. The path is soon interrupted by a ski-jump. Go down the steps, cross the jumping area and climb back to your original height to rejoin the way into the woods. Ahead is the Katrin cable-car, the summit of the Katrin (1,542 metres) an outstanding viewpoint with a choice of eating places awaiting you near the summit; one possibility for this day's walk is to confine it to a morning and spend the afternoon on the Katrin, perhaps returning by cable-car or by forest path (waymarked) in woods noted for the number of Gemse (chamois) to be seen. But give yourself time to explore Bad Ischl.

Otherwise, continue past the station and under the cable-car until, near a small waterworks building, the path bears right to join a road by garages at the outskirts of Bad Ischl. Turn right along the road but then first left along Kaltenbachstraße for some 500 metres past a holiday home. An open car park, right, gives access to a footbridge into a park. Turn left here along a tarmac path, the river now re-appearing on your right. Keep ahead across the road before veering left behind a memorial statue and continue in the same direction through the riverside park, past a playground. This soon becomes part of Bad Ischl's fashionable Traun Promenade with its footbridge, round-topped street lights, Zauner's riverside coffee house, galleries and elegant shops.

The station is at the far side of the town, bearing left at the Traun Bridge and along the main street (Pfarrgasse) - look for the Traunreiter memorial high on the wall on the corner of a supermarket as you pass. But most people will want to linger around the restaurants, coffee house, shops, and if not to taste the mineral waters in the Trinkhalle, perhaps to enjoy coffee, cake or perhaps something stronger in one of the many welcoming establishments of the Kaiser's summer resort.

WALK FOUR: BAD ISCHL - LANGWIES - 15km (9 miles). Moderate - but with one climb of about 200 metres (600 feet) over a kilometre.

Starting Point: Bad Ischl Station (öBB).

Finishing Point: Langwies Station.

Motorists: Park in Bad Ischl and return by train. Parking restricted at Langwies.

Refreshments: Bad Ischl; Mitterweißenbach; Langwies.

Major attractions: Bad Ischl.

Maps Wanderkarte 18; F&B WK282

From Bad Ischl Station turn right out of the station drive, away from the town centre, past the Kur Hotel and parallel to the railway. Do not go over the iron bridge over the railway ahead but bear left along the Linz/Salzburg road, then bear

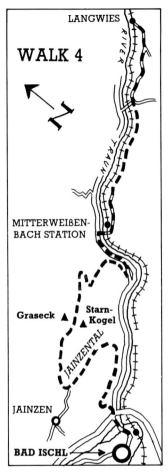

right over the concrete bridge over the River Ischl. At the first junction by the exit sign from Bad Ischl cross the road with care, following the green signs 'Spazierweg an den Jainzen' on the left which leads to a pedestrian way under the road bridge. Bear right under a tunnel. At the next junction keep ahead on the tarmac path marked 'Rund um Jainzen'. Where this

53

The Emperor's Villa with Bad Ischl in the background.

tarmac path bends left towards a house, look for another green sign 'um den Jainzen' on the right - a narrow gravel path through pasture which emerges at a farm. Keep ahead on the broad gravel track up the valley between farm buildings and houses. Keep on the main path avoiding private drives which branch off left and right, soon going alongside a small stream. Keep following the Jainzen or Jainzental signs.

Follow this main path as it bears left past car restriction signs, the path narrowing past a farmhouse to a beautiful narrow way through the forest, alongside a stream, the Jainzen Bach.

You will soon pass a small memorial plinth, deep in the forest, placed there to commemorate the place where Crown Prince Rudolph, heir to the Hapsburg Empire and the Emperor's only son, shot his first deer in 1867. It was this Crown Prince Rudolph who some years later was the subject of the tragic Mayerling Affair when he was found the victim of double suicide.

Plaque commemorating Prince Rudolph's first trophy.

Keep ahead, the path now joining a quiet farm road in the Jainzental or Jainzen Valley, a favourite hunting area of the Emperor and where Empress Elisabeth, a keep fit fanatic, went on regular exercise runs from the summer palace. The road now enters a slightly broader valley of open pasture and leads to the hamlet of Jainzen where, at a chapel and school, there is a crossroads, with a track to the right signed to Satte-dau and Mitterweißbach.

Take this way right, climbing uphill on a winding track into the forest, under pylons, curving to the right before crossing a stream at a footbridge - look for the red and white waymark on the tree at the next bend.

This track joins a broad forest road (Forststraße). Turn right here, through the barrier.

This is now the start of a steady climb out of Jainzental and up through a narrow side valley with fine forest views as you ascend. Sattedau (not marked on the map) is a saddle or pass between two typical conical, forest-covered peaks, Starnkogel and Graseck. This is a steady, rather than steep ascent, rewarded by those views, past a sequence of waterfalls.

At the summit there is a junction at a tiny shrine. Turn right here, past the shrine, over the summit, but immediately past the summit is a small limestone quarry. Should a warning siren sound or red flag be in evidence keep well back from what has created a spectacular but dangerous landslip not far from the path. If all is quiet, proceed quickly past, the main path bearing left away from the quarry, downhill, with splendid views into the Traun Valley again as you emerge down the track.

This way proceeds along a great descending curve, tightening to a sharp hairpin bend before dropping down in the other direction above Mitterwießenbach. Follow this way down until it reaches the valley bottom and join a quiet track parallel to but behind the main road up the valley. Turn left here for another half kilometre until the road is reached. Cross carefully to the footpath by the opposite side and continue for a kilometre to the bridge near Mitterweißenbach Station - though if you need refreshment there is a restaurant in the village ahead.

Otherwise, turn left following the road past the station, continuing as it narrows by farms, orchards, houses alongside the railway, winding pleasantly on the valley edge - easy, pleasant walking.

The track eventually reaches a level crossing. Keep ahead, now along another stretch of forest road, a track which goes deep into the woods, ascending slightly to give intriguing glimpses of the peaks of the Gasskogel and Traunstein above the Traunsee. Keep ahead past crossing tracks and paths coming in from Bromberg Alm until you come out of the forest and reach a group of cottages in the clearing. An obvious track forks left down to the little station at Langwies.

If you find you have to wait long for a train, Gasthof Langwies with refreshments is about ten minutes' walk away - through the pedestrian tunnel under the railway and over the wooden bridge over the river, then some 100 metres to the right along the main road.

WALK FIVE: LANGWIES - EBENSEE/TRAUNKIRCHEN
9km (5½ miles)

Starting Point: Langwies Station (öBB).

Finishing Point: Ebensee Landungsplatz Station or Traunkirchen Ort Station.

Motorists: Park Ebensee and take the train to Langwies (limited parking at Langwies).

Major attractions: Ebensee with local (Heimat) Museum; Traunsee and ferry to Traunkirchen or Gmunden. Wild Park Hochkreut near Gmunden where animals wander freely in alpine setting.

Maps: Wanderkarte 18; F&B WK282

This is an easy half-day walk which means that it will leave plenty of time to explore Ebensee town and take the Traunsee boat to Traunkirchen with its spectacular setting and two beautiful churches and perhaps even explore Gmunden.

From Langwies Station go down the steps at the Bad Ischl end of the platform leading to a tunnel under the railway line before crossing the river over a wooden bridge. Turn left along the main road for 50 metres before crossing to a narrow drive leading past a traffic restriction sign to three houses, behind the first of which runs the Soleleitungsweg.

Though the Soleleitungsweg does in fact run all the way from Ischl, before Langwies it runs too close to the modern road or is too overgrown to be of much interest to walkers, but beyond Langwies it once again forms an attractive pedestrian way, a raised green path above the fields.

It is easily recognisable. You follow it first of all by telephone

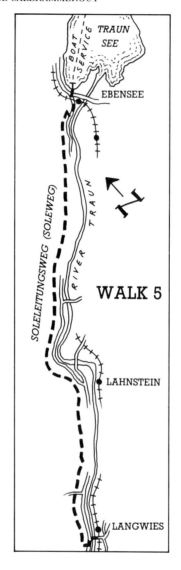

wires, behind a sawmill. It's a little overgrown, with longish grass, but easy enough to follow except where it goes behind Gasthof Langwies (refreshments) where a patch of nettles and briars forms a real barrier to all but the bold - this can be avoided by using an adjacent farm track. Beyond the Gasthof it becomes a grass and tarmac track then lane, again with traffic restriction signs, then thins to a delightful green way along the edge of a long meadow, swinging away from the road and the noisy traffic.

It is this meadow which gives Langwies its name - literally meaning 'Long Meadow'. The way goes through an improvised wire gate (close carefully) by a barn, curving back towards the road past a second cafe. Keep ahead, always looking for the linear mound which forms the Soleleitungsweg. The way eventually curves left along the edge of a wood still past this long meadow, through tall farm gates - please close them behind you. Soon after the second gate it joins a farm track leading into a hamlet which a sign on a barn, left, announces as Verteiler Vordernberg. As the farm track bends to the road, look for the path left by a telegraph pole and small building. This goes past a house and again emerges at the main road at a busy junction.

Keep left, following the line of the old road, bearing left again in front of a farmhouse where a sign announcing the Soleweg (Path no.1) puts you back on the salt pipeline behind a tall wooden barn. The track soon becomes a green path between cottages and broadens to become a lovely stretch of path curving round the hillside under a steep cliff face, left, that forms the edge of the Höllengebirge - the mountains of Hell. The edges of the path are, in mid-summer, scented with thyme and filled with harebells.

Keep ahead through another woodland section, over a footbridge and past a small waterfall. As the wood thins out you enjoy a view through the gap in the mountains to the right, across the valley, the great massif of the Totes Gebirge where a pass, clearly visible as you look across, leads to the Offensee.

This is good, easy walking, well signed either as the Soleweg or to Ebensee, even with the occasional bench to remind you that civilisation is at hand. The motor road - a quiet lane - parallels the Soleleitungsweg by Steinkogel and Plankau, and for the next three kilometres or so the way, still in woods, is above gardens. Avoid the branching path over the bridge to Ebensee town centre (mainly industrial) but keep on the Soleweg as it follows the edge of the town, the great Ebensee salt and chemical works - with its crossed hammer logo - soon coming into view, the destination for the brine from the mines above Hallstatt.

The Soleweg skirts the edge of the town, between garden and woodland. As you approach the top of the lake, the houses get closer together, and the way descends to the very backs of houses, more like an alleyway, almost in the very kitchens and sculleries that crowd round the Soleweg as it enters Ebensee, until it finally becomes a narrow street, almost Mediterranean in flavour, in the old town itself. You emerge in the Market Street full of small shops - turn right to the junction into the High Street from there go left to an attractive little park, the surprisingly modern Landungsplatz Station and either cross the main road by the station or (preferably) under the pedestrian tunnel to the left (just beyond the park) which leads to the Traunsee boat terminus and lakeside cafes.

But the old part of the Ebensee town, up the Langbathbach, with the church and Heimat (Folk) Museum are well worth exploring. If it's a fine, hot day you might be tempted to walk the kilometre or so along the Langbathsee road to the Feuerkogel cable-car up to the summit of the mountain with easy walks to nearby peaks, alpenrosen and glorious views. A no less splendid experience, in a different way, is to take the Traunsee boat to Traunkirchen, a little rocky peninsula into the lake with the Traunkirche itself, a superb baroque church famous throughout Austria for its Fischerkanzel, a brilliantly executed pulpit showing the apostles, as fishermen, hauling in their catch. The pulpit is crowned by the figure of St. Francis Xavier, the Jesuits' most famous missionary to India and Japan. The story goes than on one of his journeys, a huge storm arose and to calm the raging waters he put his crucifix among the waves only to find it dashed from his hand. When he later did land safely, a gigantic crab holding the crucifix in its pincers appeared - a story commemorated on the roof of the pulpit with a more elegant looking lobster in place of the original squat-shaped crustacean.

Find time, too, to visit the tiny ancient chapel of St. John, reached by a winding path through the trees, which offers a magnificent view across the Traunsee to the Traunstein mountain beyond. There is some evidence that it may stand on the site of a Roman building, perhaps a temple, and legend has it that it might also have been the stronghold of lake robbers or pirates.

The Traunsee, one of the most spectacularly beautiful of the Salzkammergut lakes, is also noted for its excellent fish - Forelle (trout), Reinanke and Saibling. More than 30 tonnes of fish are caught in the lake each year.

It's about a ten minute walk back from the Traunkirchen landing stage through the village to Traunkirchen Ort Station - an unstaffed halt - for trains back to Langwies, Ischl, Gmunden or Bad Aussee.

WALK SIX: TRAUNKIRCHEN/HAUS HOISERN - GMUNDEN 18km (12 miles) Strenuous

Starting Point: Haus Hosiern landing stage on the east shores of the Traunsee. This can be reached by means of the Traunsee boat from Ebensee Landungsplatz, Traunkirchen Ort (both with connecting öBB train services on the Salzkammergut line nearby), or from Gmunden.

Finishing Point: Gmunden town centre (Tram connection to Gmunden Hauptbahnhof).

Motorists: Park in Gmunden and take the boat to Haus Hoisern.

Major attractions: Laudachsee, Märchenpfad, Gmunden.

Refreshments: Haus Hoisern; Moaristidl (lakeside); Mair Alm; Gasthof Ramsau Laudachsee; Grünberg; Gmunden.

Maps: Wanderkarte 18; F&B WK282

This walk involves an extremely steep descent over the Hohe Scharte Pass including a short stretch of scrambling (with wire

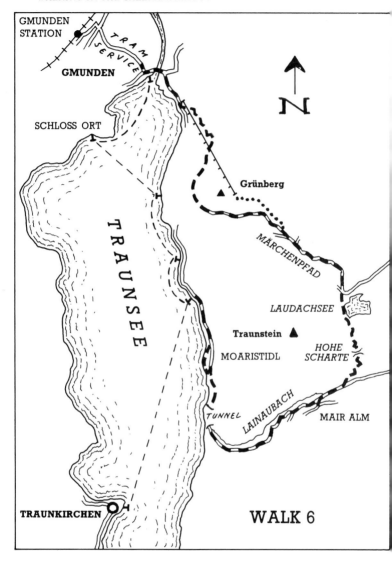

rope supports) - no more difficult than parts of the Lake District or Snowdonia, but not suitable for anyone who is not agile or without a head for heights.

You can avoid the scramble by a) returning from Mair Alm to Haus Hoisern, from thence by boat or lakeside road to Gmunden or b) by ascending the track which runs direct from Haus Hoisern to Laudachsee.

The walk can also be shortened and a steep descent avoided by taking the Grünberg cable-car from the summit of Grünberg to Gmunden.

Easy or wet weather alternatives: Follow the lakeside road from Haus Hoisern into Gmunden - tarmac road with light traffic but good lakeside views (5km). Take the Grünberg cabin-lift to the summit and then the fairly level track (signed) to Laudachsee (9km return).

From Haus Hoisern landing stage turn right into the lakeside road following it for just over a kilometre to where it terminates at a car park. Keep ahead through the car park, following the Moaristidl sign which leads to a narrow path between houses, soon going to the lakeside and winding between tall hedges to reach the Moaristidl cafe - a tempting point to stop for refreshment before the climbing ahead.

Continue along the path (or up the steps from the cafe if you call there) to where it reaches a lane. Go right for a short way but follow it left as it hairpins uphill and swings back right to cross a ravine over a concrete bridge. Keep ahead through the red barriers of a Forststraße - a pedestrian way goes to the left of the barrier. The track soon reaches and enters the Miesweg Tunnels, a series of tunnels through the limestone first built in 1878 and restored in 1979. The first tunnel is lit by a gap in its side. You come into the open air, a fine viewpoint to your right over the lake, soon climbing back into the next tunnel and emerging at a bend.

You emerge at a concrete bridge. The track now swings left through a deep, thickly forested gorge - the Lainau Bach winds in the valley below, perilously narrow pinnacles of limestone soar above, forming the southern bastions of the Traunstein mountain. The climb is gentle but steady - but keep a wary eye for falling stones.

The ascent is around 3 kilometres long. As you reach the summit of the gorge, keep ahead past a track coming in from the left. A barn on the right indicates the way (signed) to Mair Alm, a delightful and typical mountain Alm offering for all but the most stoic an excellent place to stop for lunch or 'Jause'.

Cross back down to the main track from Mair Alm, and continue eastwards for just less than a kilometre to where a forest path clearly waymarked and signed 'Laudachsee - Traxenbichel' bears off left. This is an extremely steep but clear path, Gassner Steig, well waymarked, through the woods, zig-zagging uphill, stones and tree roots like steps. Take your time as there are about 300 metres (1,000 feet) of ascent. You reach a broad and fairly recent forest track. Cross, and look for the continuation of the path half-left back into the trees - a waymark will confirm the way uphill.

You finally reach the summit of the pass - the Hohe Scharte, 'the High Fissure', 1,113 metres above sea level and with a superb view of Laudachsee below you, and the Katzenstein (1,349) with its summit cross the craggy peak to your right. It was from here that the Giant Erla gazed down on the water nymph Blondchen in the lake below - see the folk tale recounted at the end of this walk.

Take great care with the descent. This is a short but steep scramble down rocky steps, with twin wire ropes to hold firmly onto. It is perfectly safe - but not to be hurried. In the steepest stretches it is easier to come down backwards, clinging to the ropes but seeking firm footholds. After 50 metres or so the gradient eases and the path becomes a normal, steeply zig-zagging path through the woods. Follow it down to a junction with a track. Bear left for Laudachsee.

After the exertions and the excitements of climb and descent, you'll probably want to enjoy a few minutes' rest by the lake, perhaps even with a long or strong drink from the cafe. This is a particularly fine mountain lake, with the Katzenstein's steep pyramid sharply reflected in the lake water, and an alpine meadow in the foreground.

From the Ramsau Alm take the main track left signed Grün-

Märchenpfad - the end of Walk 6

berg Seilbahn. This is a broad forest track and 'Waldpferd-pfad' with a series of signboards about the forest and individual trees. Even more interesting is the 'Märchenpfad' - 'Folk Tale Path' or Trail - a series of enchanting wooden sculptures in the forest, culminating in a little stream-powered xylophone whose melody echoes through the woods, the carvings of the Giant Erla and the witch Kranawitha, and the Seven Springs of the Seven Brothers; all illustrating folk stories which are actually set in the vicinity. Two of the most important and romantic of the tales are related at the end of this section.

You come to an important junction of tracks. If you have decided to take the Grünberg cabin-car, follow the Seilbahn signs, second left, (last descent in the summer months 6.00pm.) to a narrow woodland way which climbs gently to the cable-car terminus.

Otherwise, take the first track left signed W8 to Hotel Ramsau but then at the next junction, go right, signed for Gmunden (a small sign) - path W7. This becomes a broader forest track, ascending slightly but then contouring around the

65

hillside and descending by tall fir trees to give several magnificent panoramas as the forest opens out. With the great peak of the Traunstein behind you, you look across the Traunsee to Altmunster, Traunkirchen, Ebensee.

The way continues to curve around until the views are now forward across to Schloss Ort, the little island castle near Gmunden, Gmunden town itself, and the flat lands to the north and beyond Vöcklabruck which stretch out before you - an astonishing contrast to the mountains to the south.

There is a romantic but true story connected with the lake castle or Seeschloss Ort which belonged to Archduke Johann Salvator, a nephew of the Emperor Franz Joseph and close friend of Crown Prince Rudolf of Habsburg. In 1889 the Archduke renounced his title and married the actress Milly Stübel, taking the name of Johann Orth and leaving Europe intending to emigrate to South America. But sadly he never arrived - his ship would appear to have been overtaken by storms. Some time later a rusty Austrian revolver was found next to a skeleton on a remote island in the Indian Ocean. Whether that was the former Archduke or what indeed had happened to him will never be known.

You soon reach the Grünberg cable-car, just past which there is a crossing of paths where the direct waymarked route down to Gmunden, Ortner Steig, bears left. This is a steep, narrow way with some awkward muddy stretches before it bears right along a narrow enclosed way which goes below the Moosberg Hotel, turning left down side roads to the lake shore. Rather than the steep Ortner Steig, it is a little easier on the knees to retain height for another 600 metres before taking the next less steep path left which passes the Hotel Moos for the lake shore.

Follow the lake (a shore promenade runs most of the way) to the Traun Bridge and into the town centre.

Gmunden - the end of the 'Salzkammergut Way' - has much to revive the spirits of even the weariest walker - lake views, boats, cafes, cake shops, promenades, parks; this is a handsome lake resort which has grown out of a medieval town and important administrative centre and depot of the salt industry.

Schloss Ort, Gmunden

You'll even see a bronze sculpture of a salt miner with a large rock crystal poised above him to represent salt in the centre of a fountain along the promenade and not far from the main square. You'll also find a memorial to composer Franz Schubert who stayed here during the summer of 1825.

An excellent museum in the old Kammerhof - which dates back to the 15th century - illustrates many aspects of the industry and its workers, and contains samples of the distinctive hand-painted Gmunden pottery as well as memorabilia of Johannes Brahms and the philosopher Hebbel.

Katzenstein and Laudachsee. Note the profile of the 'Sleeping Grecian Girl', if the photo is looked at vertically - the peak is the nose, lips below, then chin and neck.

The 16th century Town Hall - Rathaus - overlooking the square has a rare ceramic carillon of bells that play Schubert and Bruckner on the hour. You'll find narrow winding streets and courtyards, salt merchant's houses, wine and beer cellars, a magnificent baroque church, shops, cafes and Konditorei to rival those of Bad Ischl.

The little tram that climbs up to the station leaves Franz Joseph Platz (the main street on the south side of the Town Hall) and meets trains to and from Bad Ischl and Bad Aussee, but check departure times on the notice-board by the terminus as the timetable in the evening is somewhat irregular.

THE STORY OF GIANT ERLA AND THE WATER NYMPH FROM THE LAUDACHSEE

(A characteristic of these two Salzkammergut folk tales is how they weave into and explain the natural phenomenon of the landscape, including features actually passed on this walk.)

On a high hill over the Traunsee lived Giant Erla, a good-natured soul who was liked by all. One evening in the moonlight, he saw a beautiful water nymph whose hair shone like gold. Night after night the giant sat on the pass between the Traunstein and Katzenstein mountains and watched her bathing, and because of her golden hair, he named her Blondchen. The water nymph liked the good-natured giant who so obviously admired her and who promised her a beautiful castle.

He started to carry out his plans by bringing blocks of stone from the Traunstein rocks and threw them into the lake to make an island. He also uprooted trees for building materials and obtained marble from the Dachstein mountains and gold and precious stones from the mines. He was aided in his work by King Rötel's dwarfs and soon a splendid castle was constructed. Blondchen was delighted, but Giant Erla was too big to enter it. In despair he turned to the witch Kranawitha from the Höllengebirge for help. She changed him into a handsome knight and after great wedding festivities, Blondchen and the knight moved into the castle and were very happy.

As the seasons changed to autumn with its mists, Blondchen became ill and by the time the snows came, the lovely water nymph was dead. The knight was inconsolable and mourned his dead love. A little boat rowed by the dwarfs came over the lake from the Traunstein and carried Blondchen's coffin to the Laudachsee. The waves gleamed silver in the moonlight and the coffin shimmered as it sank in the lake. To this day fishermen and hunters say that they sometimes see a strange light in the depth of the lake at full moon.

The knight disappeared and the witch broke the spell. After some time, the noise of hammering filled the air and Giant Erla was discovered to have modelled Blondchen's likeness in the rocks. A glance at the skyline along the Traunsee will show to this day the classical profile of a beautiful young woman asleep - 'Die schlafende Griechin'.

THE TALE OF THE SEVEN SPRINGS

Long ago there lived a fierce and ruthless king who forbade anyone to enter his hunting territory. He had seven sons whom he idolised and who lived in his large hunting lodge. One day he met an old woman in difficulties who had fallen off the Traunstein mountain and had somehow managed to drag herself as far as the king's territory. She asked him to help her, but he refused furiously and lunged at her as if to kill her. Then the earth shook and a terrible curse came from the old woman's mouth. The king in consternation recognised the witch Kranawitha in disguise.

Kranawitha hit the rocks seven times with a stick and seven natural springs appeared, then she grinned mockingly at him and disappeared. Sick at heart, the king rushed to his hunting lodge to find his sons, but in vain. The witch had punished him by changing his sons into springs welling up from the ground.

Racked with grief, the king went up to the Traunstein and you can still hear him weeping and complaining, but his sons still wait to be awakened from their enchantment.

PART THREE - SEVEN LAKELAND WALKS IN THE SALZKAMMERGUT

WALK SEVEN: THE HALLSTÄTTERSEE
OSTUFER WAY 8km (5 miles) Easy

Starting Point: Steeg Gosau Station (öBB)

Finishing Point: Hallstatt Station (öBB) for lake ferry to town. Return can also be made by Postbus 2572 direct from Hallstatt to Steeg Gosau Station.

Motorists: Park at Steeg Gosau Station and return by train or bus.

Refreshments: Steeg Gosau Dreimädlerhaus; Untersee (Gasthof Ebner); Gasthof Tuscher by lakeside near Obertraun Station; Hallstatt Station; Hallstatt.

Major attractions: Hallstatt.

Maps: Wanderkarte 20; F&B WK281

We make no apologies for including yet another walk by the Hallstätter See. This is an exceptionally beautiful walk and will combine perfectly with an afternoon visit to Hallstatt with its many treasures, including the Salt Mines; alternatively this can be combined with Walk One for a through route to Obertraun or as a low level alternative to Walk Two.

From Steeg Gosau Station follow the handsome wooden Ostufer (East Bank) Wanderweg signs left to the main road by the level crossing. Cross both road then railway and then take the path right by the railway which swings round to join a narrow lane. Turn right again here along the lane which goes parallel to and under the railway before reaching a crossroads at Untersee. Turn right here but take the first lane left (signed) by Gasthaus Ebner. After about 250 metres turn right along a narrow track which leads under the railway before turning left parallel to the line and by open meadows, soon crossing to the lakeside and passing by scattered farms and outbuildings. This is easy, gentle walking with increasingly impressive views of the Hallstättersee. You will be able to make out the line of the

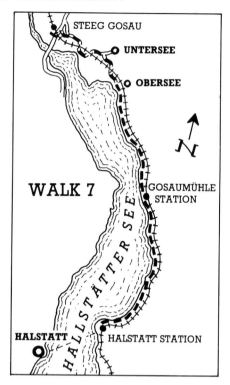

Soleleitungsweg along the forested hillside (Walk Two), and see the Gosauzwang bridge across the side valley.

Continue for the next two kilometres, the way gently curving round between railway line and lake, close to the lake edge, by Obersee Station and the lakeside Gasthof Tuscher, an excellent point for refreshment in a superb setting with some local farm-house specialities on offer for guests.

The lakeside path continues, soon entering a long, narrow bend, at one point climbing close to the railway line through a turnstile, and forming a Nature Trail with carefully labelled plants and trees, and increasingly thrilling views across the lake with Hallstatt town in its astonishing lake and mountain

Futteraffen in the forest

setting directly ahead.

As you approach the curve of the headland, the path is purely artificial, a wooden walkway built out onto the lake as recently as the mid-1980s - you'll see a memorial plaque to the late Willi Kirschlager (1916-85) to whose inspiration we owe this route.

You cross a magnificently engineered footbridge dizzily suspended over lake and below railway line, before the path winds by cliff and railway into Hallstatt Station itself, from where the ferry boat leaves at regular intervals before and after the departure of trains. The station buffet serves light refreshments if you need to wait for boat or train.

Alternatively you might like to continue on the Ostufer Weg by lakeside path and nature trail to Obertraun (Walk One).

A visit to Hallstatt should include the parish church, originally late Romanesque in style with frescoes over the entrance, depicting scenes of the Crucifixion from an unknown master of the Danube school. These have of course been much restored. A winged altar from the sixteenth century by Leonhard Astl, a worthy disciple of Michael Pacher (see Walk Eleven, Wolfgangsee) is again a masterpiece which took nearly a decade 1510-1520 to complete. One has to admire also the sense of drama that the winged style of altar helped to promote so that particular sections could be opened or closed for special church festivals such as Advent, Christmas and Lent. A neo-gothic altar from 1870 is another splendid feature.

Hallstatt only had its own parish priest from about the year 1400, so it was also the custom to put a light outside the church on a high point whenever a priest arrived from Goisern to hold divine service to attract a congregation of the faithful.

Just through the churchyard is the little building which houses the Ossuary or Bonehouse and contains about 1,200 skulls and other human bones. What makes this place so renowned is the ancient custom of painting the skulls with the name of the deceased, their dates and even their status. Women are usually given flower garlands as decoration and men, oak or ivy leaves. The custom arose from the fact that space in the little churchyard was so limited that remains were dug up after a ten or twelve year period to provide space for new tenants. Nowadays, the custom still continues, but only if expressly willed by the departed or near relatives.

It is a place which may well prove upsetting for some visitors, so please make this visit optional. It is nevertheless a moving experience to look upon those frail and vulnerable relics in such a place of vivid beauty and life as Hallstatt is, a reminder of the transience of all things.

WALK EIGHT: ALTAUSSEER SEE - 9km (5½ miles) Easy

Starting Point: Bus terminus at the Kurhaus, Altaussee. This can be reached by catching Postbus 6844 (approximately hourly) which meets trains at Bad Aussee Station and serves Bad Aussee town centre (Post Office).

Finishing Point: As above.

Motorists: Park in Altaussee.

Refreshments: Altaussee town; the Strandcafe (southern shore) noted for its excellent fish dishes; Fischerndorf (north shore).

Major attractions: Altaussee Local Museum (in Kurhaus); Altausseer Lake; the Altaussee Salt Mines which can be reached along a 3km (2 mile) footpath route from Altaussee. A visit to the salt mines can therefore be very conveniently combined with the circular walk around the lake. This is an excellent - and contrasting - day of anyone's holiday.

Maps: Wanderkarte 20; F&B WK281

Altaussee town is a small, lakeside spa and resort on the western edge of this magnificent Alpine lake, in the centre of what is known as 'Ausseerland': the region of the Saltzkammergut in Styria, to the north of Bad Aussee itself. During the summer months the Postbus from Bad Aussee continues from Altauseer Lake over the serpentine Maitstraße Pass to the Loser Hut on Loser (1,838m), an outlying bastion of the Totes Gebirge and a magnificent viewpoint.

Late May is the time of year when all the hillside slopes around the Altausseer and other lakes in the area are covered with thousands and thousands of pure white scented narcissus at a time when many of the topmost peaks still have their coating of snow. In late May a Narzissenfest takes place on the Altausseer - Austria's largest flower festival, a three day event with parades and processions consisting of decorated boats and vehicles incorporating these beautiful flowers.

The Kurhaus has an Information Centre and an interesting

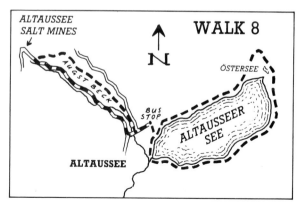

museum of the spa and of some of its more distinguished liter-
ary visitors (open weekdays 10.00-12.00 only, Saturdays
4.00pm-6.00pm).

If you decide to visit the salt mines on foot, walk through the
little park at the side of the Kurhaus, at the end of which a path
bears left by gardens to join the lane to Loser Hut. At the
bridge over the Augst Beck turn left but turn first right along a
narrow lane by houses and gardens which soon becomes a path
marked to Blea Alm. Follow the path up the narrow valley
through woods and across meadows which after about 1½km
from the bridge descends to a cluster of farm buildings and a
junction of paths where a narrow way, left signed to 'Salzberg'
climbs uphill by pylons into the forest. Take this way, a steep
ascent through the woods with a stream to your left. Keep on
in the same direction until the path, a little overgrown,
emerges at a track by a (closed) mine entrance. Bear right past
this mine building, again climbing uphill until you join the
road just below the public entrance to the Altaussee Salt
Mines. Notices in the window announce the time of tours
(basically hourly) and there is a cafeteria by the entrance.

This is both a mine (which has been in operation since 1143
AD and still produces over a million cubic metres of brine per
annum) and a museum and among its most spectacular features
are an underground salt lake where extraordinary lighting
effects are demonstrated, polished wooden slides down which
visitors hurtle between levels and the Saint Barbara Salt Chapel
with an altar of illuminated transparent salt crystals. Saline
levels in the cave atmosphere preserve fir branches kept
around the little shrine for a year or more - but they quickly
crumble when taken into the fresh air.

Return to Altaussee along the lane to avoid the steep path
downhill.

The walk around Altausseer See begins at the Kurpark and bus
terminus. Take the path directly ahead across the meadow and
towards the lake marked with a circular no traffic sign which
soon becomes a grassy path by a hockey pitch and hang-gliding
landing area, with spectacular views to your right towards the
Dachstein range. The path bears left by two little wooden

fieldbarns to join the main (tarmac) lakeside path. Turn right here by tennis courts and the Hotel Seevilla where a plaque on the wall will inform you no less a figure than Johannes Brahms - a frequent visitor to Ausseerland for the summer air - came here in 1882 to give the world première of two of his most celebrated chamber works.

Another composer to visit Altaussee was Gustav Mahler who wrote the opening movements of his Fourth Symphony whilst staying near the lake.

At the bridge bear left with the 'Weg um den See' signs along the lakeside crowded with boats, boat-houses and landing stages, and the Restaurant Strand Cafe, noted for its excellent lake trout. You soon reach a junction of ways; keep to the left-hand path 'Ufer Promenade um den See', now entering a 'Naturschutzgebiet' or nature reserve.

This then becomes an exquisitely beautiful path by the lake shore, frequently punctuated by little bays and benches where you can sit and gaze across the water to where the green hillside and bare summit of Loser Mountain are reflected, mirror-like in the stillness of the lake beyond. This is not a walk to hurry.

It is also an extremely popular path where you are as much likely to meet elderly Viennese ladies in fashionable dirndls, stout walking shoes and elegant walking stick umbrellas as the more orthodox hiker in sweatshirt and shorts. Everyone in Austria takes 'Wandern' as their birthright.

The path is easy to follow and skirts the lake, gradually swinging northwards around the head of the lake, before curving away (keep to the main path) through marshy land past and behind the tiny half-hidden Östersee deep in the woods, its name 'Easter Lake' denoting the fact that it re-appears each year as the lake levels rise with the melting spring snows of Easter.

At the junction with the mountain path from Wildensee Hut, turn left back to the lake shore, the views now dominated by the Trisselwand crags to the east. This is another superb stretch of path sometimes close to the edge of the water, sometimes more elevated. Soon past a bridge and little wooden shelter the path becomes a track past the Jausenstation

Freibad, leading into Fischerndorf with its cafes and hotels. Look for the path, left, reached past the Hotel am See, named the Johannes Brahams Promenade, recalling that great master's frequent walks by this shore, which goes past hotels, boat-houses to where, near the little barns, your fieldpath leads back up to the Kurhaus.

WALK NINE: GRUNDLSEE, TOPLITZSEE AND KAMMERSEE - 12km (8 miles) Easy

Starting Point: Grundlsee landing stage (Seeklause). This is served by Postbus 6840 direct from Bad Aussee Station and town centre.

Finishing Point: Gössl landing place for Grundlsee boat (or bus direct to Bad Aussee).

Motorists: Park in Grundlsee town (lakeside car parking) and return from Gößl by boat - or bus.

Refreshments: In Grundlsee; the Rostiger Ankar by lakeside at Gößl; Jausenstation at Toplitzsee.

Major attractions: All three lakes, including gondola service to Kammersee; Bad Aussee.

Maps: Wanderkarte 20; F&B WK281

This walk might well be combined with a visit to Bad Aussee - an attractive town and resort with medieval (late Gothic) houses, a 14th century church with a fine altarpiece of the 15th century, a local museum in the Kammerhof - the former Salt Office.

Bad Aussee was the home of Anna Plochl (1804-85), the local postmaster's daughter who married Archduke Johann (1782-1859) and became Countess of Meran. Their long courtship with the many problems such differing rank brought, is a fascinating and romantic - and perfectly true - story. Such were Anna's exceptional qualities that she was later to win grudging acceptance in court circles.

You'll see the Archduke's statue in the Kurpark and a medallion depicting the Duke and Anna on the Erzhog Johann Bridge across the River Traun.

For the walk around the Grundlsee, take Postbus 6840 from

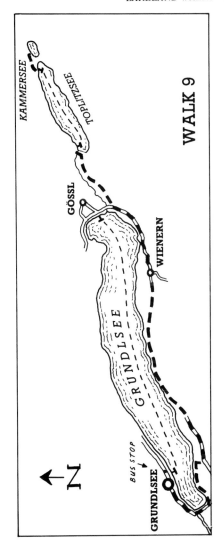

Boats on Toplitzsee

Bad Aussee and alight near the first landing stage - at See-klause.

Follow the main road back towards Bad Aussee to the foot of the lake crossing the bridge over the River Traun and then turn left before Gasthof Seeblick along a track signed Wanderweg No.1 to Gössl.

Bear left at a fork of tracks, again following the Gössl signs towards the lake. Keep ahead, ignoring a crossing path, along a path through a meadow. At the next junction keep right uphill towards a wood for around 100 metres, before going left at the junction along the farm track past Mitterau, enjoying panoramic views across Grundlsee and the mountain ranges of the Totes Gebirge beyond - Tressel Kogel, The Beckstein and The Rechenstein are the impressive peaks in the foreground.

The track soon thins to become, beyond Hinterau, a narrow but very easy to follow woodland path along a steeply wooded hillside, with superb views of the lake through the trees from the shelf-like path.

This is all delightful walking, before the way eventually ascends to join a forest road leading into the hamlet of Wienern, past some attractive, unspoiled traditionally decorated farmhouses. It broadens to a tarmac road by the Postbus terminus (from where if circumstances dictate, you can catch the Postbus 6840 directly to Bad Aussee).

Follow the lane as it curves gradually down to the lakeside to the head of the lake from where you'll enjoy fine lakeside views and, at the Rostiger Ankar, excellent traditional Salzkammergut food and drink in simple but traditional surroundings.

For the path to Toplitzsee cross the road and retrace your steps a short way from the Rostiger Ankar to join a track, left, signed 'Wanderweg 4 zum Toplitzsee'. This soon reaches a forest track barrier. Do not take the track which forks left into a quarry, but keep ahead, slightly right, past the barrier, signed Alexander Baumann-Weg, soon climbing uphill through the forest.

You eventually reach a T-junction into a broader track. Turn right here to follow this track which soon reaches the shore of the beautiful, hidden Toplitzsee, a mountain lake with a Jausenstation (cafe). During the main season, motorised gondolas take you across the still waters of the little lake, at the head of which you are landed to take the short walk up the steps and over the headland to the Kammersee, a tiny, circular lake surrounded by peaks, where you'll see the cascade down the hillside which forms the source of the River Traun. This trip is not to be missed for the beauty of the scenery and the atmosphere of the two top lakes that form the source of the Traun - an important tributary of the Danube that runs to Vienna and eventually to the Black Sea.

As you return on the boat across the Toplitzsee, reflect that it was apparently in these dark waters that millions of pounds of carefully forged English money, created by Nazi forgers during the last war, was hidden. It was designed to be brought over to Britain in vast quantities to ruin the British economy. According to local wisdom it still remains hidden here.

From the landing area, take the broader track to the right, Wanderweg 3, which leads directly past a beautiful little

Kammersee

baroque wayside chapel, back to Gössl at the head of the lake from where the Grundlsee boat takes you back to the foot of the lake - a trip every bit as lovely as the walk.

If you've time to wait, refreshment is available at the Gasthof two minutes' walk from the landing stage; there's also the bus stop close by for the direct Postbus service around the lake and back to Bad Aussee.

WALK TEN: GOSAUSEE - 14km (8 miles) Moderate

Starting Point: Gosausee car park and bus terminus. This is reached by Postbus 2570 which links with trains from Bad Ischl and Steeg Gosau stations.

Finishing Point: Gosausee car park.

Motorists: Gosausee car park, signed from Gosau.

Refreshments: Restaurant at the Gosaukammbahn cable-car station; Holzmeisteralm at the head of the Hinterer Gosausee.

Major attractions: The Dachstein views from both lakes; Gosaukammbahn cable-car.

Maps: Wanderkarte 20; F&B WK281

This is one of the most famous and spectacular walks in the Salzkammergut, with breathtaking - and much photographed - views of the Dachstein glacier reflected in the still waters of the two Alpine lakes. For this reason, if no other, save this walk for a fine day when clear skies and sunlight provide the clarity to enjoy this astonishing landscape at its best. Low cloud and rain will obliterate more than you can afford to miss.

From the bus stop or top car park make your way up the steps by the concrete barrier to the lake shore, immediately to enjoy the famous view across the Vorderer Gosausee which, if the weather is clear, is like a great romantic painting with sky, mountain, snow, forest and lake juxtaposed in perfect harmony.

Follow the track around the left side of the lake where a sign will confirm if the Holzmeisteralm - an excellent stop for lunch or light refreshment - is open; important in an otherwise remote setting.

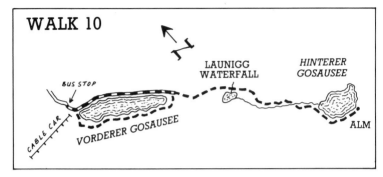

This is easy, lake shore walking, with spectacular views to enjoy behind to the great rocky ridge of the Gosaukamm, served by the cable-car.

Continue to the head of the lake from where the track enters the forest and begins to climb steadily. After about a kilometre a shallow tarn fills a hollow on the right in a clearing, again a favourite photographers' spot. You pass a little waterfall on the left, Launigg Wasserfall, the track now climbs steeply and curving round until it crests the summit and through the trees you glimpse the Hinterer Gosausee.

A viewpoint and bench at the foot of this lake is a place to sit and stare. This is, if anything, even more overpoweringly beautiful than the Vorderer Gosausee, and being away from the noise and clatter of traffic, incredibly still and quiet, the massive summit of the Dachstein, its craggy peaks and vivid white ice-cap a vision into a remote world normally only enjoyed by the climber. The lake is a large mirror, sky, forest crag and glacier and shadow captured yet subtly transformed on the surface of its mysterious green-blue water.

Follow the path round the edge of the lake to the Holz-meisteralm where you can sit indoors or out depending on the weather and your mood, to enjoy the perfect setting - and some simple, but excellent, Alpine food and drink.

Paths beyond here are mountain walks or scrambles - superb by any standards but definitely only for the experienced.

Return the same way (the views back down the valley offer

ample reward for retraced steps) - but when you reach the head
of the Vorderer Gosausee turn left along the path around the
south bank of the lake, a beautiful, winding way terraced into
the hillside which soon emerges at the lakefoot promenade for
cafe, shops, and bus terminus or car.

WALK ELEVEN: WOLFGANGSEE PILGRIMS' WAY
12km (8 miles) Moderate

Starting Point: St. Wolfgang. This is reached by Postbus 2560
which operates regularly from Bad Ischl Station.

Finishing Point: St. Gilgen. A return to Bad Ischl and connections
onto the Salzkammergut railway can be made either by direct
Postbus 3000 from the Zwölferhorn cable-car station at the top end
of town, or, more romantically perhaps, by catching one of the
many Wolfgangsee Steamers from the landing stage (operated by
öBB) back to St. Wolfgang, then bus 2560 back to Ischl.

Motorists: Park in St. Wolfgang and return by boat.

Refreshments: St. Wolfgang (wide choice of cafes and restaurants);
Gasthof Fürberg (9km); St. Gilgen.

Major attractions: The Pilgrimage Church in St. Wolfgang; the
Forest Chapel; St. Gilgen Church; the Schafberg Steam Rack
Railway (St. Wolfgang-Schafberg).

Maps: Wanderkarte 18; F&B WK282

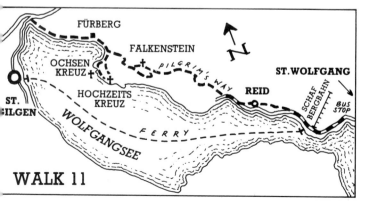

WALK 11

For most English-speaking visitors, St. Wolfgang is the most familiar part of the Salzkammergut because it is relatively close to Salzburg. It also has become well known because of the 'White Horse Inn' operetta (The 'Weisses Rössl' Gasthof still welcomes guests) and the famous view of church and town perched on the edge of the lake. It's also extremely well supplied with hotels, which makes it popular with many UK coach and package tour operators, making it the most 'British' of the Salzkammergut resorts and the one where you are likely to hear most English spoken.

It remains a charming little town, well filled with cafes, tourist shops and crowded shopping streets with boutiques. But there is more to St. Wolfgang than tourist froth.

In particular there is the 15th century 'pilgrimage' church, dedicated to St. Wolfgang of Regensburg, superbly situated above the lake side. Among many impressive features is a superb carved and painted fifteenth century altar, the work of the great sculptor Michael Pacher (*c.*1435-98). This magnificent triptych, originally designed to have its winged side pieces open only on high church festivals, is a masterpiece of late Gothic art, and was completed in 1481, the fruit of ten years' dedicated work. Almost as amazing as the altar itself is the story of the journey of the delicate and fragile work of art over the Brenner Pass by carts, boats and rafts, from South Tyrol where it was carved and painted, to its present resting place. Another splendid piece to be enjoyed in the church is Thomas Schwanthaler's baroque-style double altar of 1676.

This walk follows a route reputed to be - and almost certainly was - taken by St. Wolfgang, Bishop of Regensburg between 972 and 949 AD, in his journey from Bavaria to the church and town he established on the shore of the lake now named after him, which became a subsequent place and route of pilgrimage for medieval pilgrims in the centuries afterwards.

Follow the main street, Pilgerstraße (Pilgrim Street), from the Market Place along the promenade, past the Schafberg Railway to where the road narrows over a bridge over a stream. About 100 metres beyond this, turn right up a side road opposite a wooden information kiosk climbing up by houses to a lane at the top. Turn left here, by Gasthof Zimmerman. This becomes a narrow, tarmac lane between pasture and scattered houses, past a tiny shrine, with impressive high-level views across the lake.

At a hamlet with a scatter of houses and farms, you reach a fork - your way is left, signed to Falkenstein, descending by a house with a fine garden and ornate window-boxes to the road below, in the hamlet of Ried. Continue ahead for some 300 metres to where the road bends and a path - with a traffic no entry sign - bears off right, uphill, signed to Falkenstein and St. Gilgen. This is the Pilgrim's Way, a steep path marked every few hundred metres with exquisite little painted shrines, all linked with St. Wolfgang - to mark, among other things, points where the saint rested on his journey.

The path - waymarked as Route 28 - enters the wood and climbs steeply. Follow the red waymarks where it crosses a stream and bends sharply right uphill - avoid the temptation to go straight ahead on the more obvious path here. This path climbs uphill, with benches to afford modern pilgrims welcome rest, before swinging left again and making a steady ascent through mature forest, again passing shrines.

At the top of the hill, below the Falkenstein rock, there is a junction of ways where a steep path, signed Scheffelblick, leaves the main track left climbing uphill, along a wooden stepped walkway and narrow limestone path to the Scheffel-blick, a magnificent panoramic viewpoint across the lake.

You can either continue along the path ahead to rejoin the main Route 28, but better is to retrace your steps to explore, along the main route, the beautifully painted little shelter and shrine on the summit of the Falkenstein which shows scenes from St. Wolfgang's life, close to where the holy spring flowed from the bare rock when the saint passed.

There are a number of legends dealing with St. Wolfgang's life. One tells of the way he frustrated the devil in his attempt to throw him from a high cliff. Wolfgang's fame as a holy man spread to such an extent that he was given the bishopric, in 972, of Regensburg by Emperor Otto II.

But St. Wolfgang found that the crowded city impeded his

Forest Chapel

desire for peace and meditation. He wandered towards the Salzkammergut or the land above the River Enns with a single companion. As he looked for water one day to quench his thirst, he found a miraculous healing spring deep in the forest and resolved to stay here alone. He sent away his companion and became a hermit on the Falkenstein, among the rocks. In 976 he founded the town and church of St. Wolfgang, which became a famous centre of pilgrimage. Another story relates that Bishop Wolfgang climbed to the highest point of the Falkenstein and threw down an axe in order to build a chapel where it landed.

From here you will almost certainly hear the tolling of a bell. As you descend the origin of the sound is apparent - a little white forest chapel built into and out from the rock where, within, you will find not only a little altar and a holy well but the bell-rope which you are invited to gently ring three times - and wish, the sounds of the bell being wishes that float their way across the tree-tops.

If this was the chapel built where Wolfgang's axe landed

from the top of the Falkenstein, one can but admire his prowess. From the chapel the path is a steep descent, past more shrines including a modern series of carvings which illustrate Christ's Fourteen Stations of the Cross.

The descent ends at a crossroads. Though your way to St. Gilgen lies right via Fürberg, it is worth taking a rather special small detour via the Ochsenkreuz. Turn left along the track to yet another shrine, this time to St. Hubertus. Almost opposite, a path, Jos Eber Weg 19, leads to Ochsenkreuz and follows meadow and lakeside around the little headland. It soon leads into the wood and across a rocky point to where you look across the lake to St. Gilgen with its prominent onion-domed baroque church, with the Zwölferhorn (1,521m) in the background. In the immediate foreground is the Ochsenkreuz, a white shrine on a tiny lake islet, the lake an astonishingly rich shade of green around the shore.

Follow Path 19 on through the woods, keeping close to the shoreline where the route isn't clear, to the Hochzeitkreuz, another impressive shrine and lakeshore viewpoint, erected in 1609 by a local nobleman to commemorate his wedding.

The path returns to the main track from where you go left again to return to the Hubertus shrine and the track along the shore to Fürberg, with an imposing lakeside restaurant and boat landing stage where the walk could be terminated. Otherwise keep ahead to the left of the Gasthof along a narrow path by the lake by the water's edge, which eventually passes some fine old farmhouses and emerges at Brunnwinkl and the tarmac road. Turn left to soon reach St. Gilgen, bearing left at the junction in the town down to the church and landing stages.

St. Gilgen's greatest claim to fame perhaps is that it was the birthplace of Mozart's mother, Anna Maria Pertl (1720-78). His sister Nannerl lived here between 1784 and 1801 - you'll pass the house en route to the landing stage. It has some charming houses and a fine church, though the area around the landing stage has become somewhat commercialised. There's a good choice of places for refreshment, however, and a frequent boat service back to St. Wolfgang.

Hochzeitkreuz, Wolfgangsee

LAKELAND WALKS - WALK TWELVE

WALK TWELVE: ALONG THE ATTERSEE WESTWANDERWEG - 11km (7 miles) Moderate

Starting Point: Stockwinkl landing stage (Attersee Lake Steamers). The Attersee can be reached by Postbus 2564 direct from Bad Ischl to Unterach (Mondays to Fridays only July, August and early September), by bus 2548 from Gmunden (on Sundays only) between May and September. From Unterach a lake steamer service runs to Stockwinkl. At other times there is a öBB rail connection via Attnang Pucheim and Vöcklabruck to Kammer Schörfling (Table 17b) where trains meet boats but a change of boat is necessary onto the 'Rundkurs Süd 1' service at Attersee town across the lake. Alternatively - and this is well worth incorporating into the trip - take the train to Vöcklamarkt for the 'Attersee Bummelszug' - a private (Stern & Hafferl) narrow gauge vintage tram/light rail service (öBB tickets valid) direct to and from Attersee town, to pick up the southbound boat.

   If boats are not operating or are inconvenient, Stern & Hafferl buses operate between Unterach and Attersee - about a two hourly interval service.

Finishing Point: Nußdorf landing stage.

Motorists: Park at Nußdorf and catch the boat to Stockwinkl.

Refreshments: Lakeside restaurants at Stockwinkl and Nußdorf.

Major attractions: Lakeside steamers and 'Attersee Bummelszug' - see above. It is worth planning this walk to fit in with a train and boat journey on this remarkable local transport system, including a circular trip around the lake.

Maps: Wanderkarte 18; F&B WK282

The Attersee is the largest lake in Salzkammergut and offers enough along its extensive shores and backcloth of mountains to fill a book in its own right. It also enjoys a special place in Austrian - and European - cultural history of the 20th century, being where two of the greatest figures of their age spent creative time. The composer Gustav Mahler (1860-1911) wrote his great Third Symphony - deeply influenced by the beauty of the landscape and of nature - whilst staying at Steinbach on the Attersee in 1896. Gustav Klimt (1862-1918) the Viennese painter of the Secession Movement retreated here during

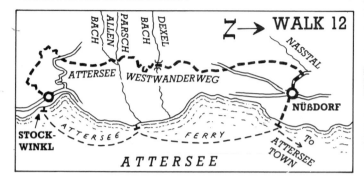

World War I and his marvellous impressionistic Attersee paintings hang in art galleries in Salzburg, Vienna and elsewhere.

This walk utilises a central portion of the 35km Attersee West Wanderweg which runs from Kammer to Unterach.

From the Stockwinkl landing stage bear left up to the main road and turn right, but almost immediately cross to locate a track on the left signed to Egelsee and Unterach. Follow the track as it ascends through a wood alongside a stream. Bear left at a junction, keeping left on a narrow path, stone surfaced, waymarked and signed to Egelsee - a superb view of the lake is now behind and to your left. At a bench, turn right on a path signed to Egelsee. Follow it by the edge of the wood. It soon narrows, plunging deep into the woods, waymarked before climbing steadily to reach a lane.

At this lane, turn right uphill - ignoring now the path that bears left to Egelsee, but climbing up some 200 metres, past a farm, to a junction. Bear right here, following the distinctive West Wanderweg sign to Nußdorf. This becomes a farm track flanked by apple and pear trees. At the farm look for the West Wanderweg Nußdorf sign, which leads to a narrow path to the left and below the farm buildings.

The path, well marked, goes deep into the wood, descending to cross a footbridge over a little ravine. At the top of the wood bear left, with the West Wanderweg signs, along a grassy path to the outside of the fir wood.

The Attersee Westwanderweg

At a curving crossing track by another sign, turn right towards the road. Note a house with a red roof ahead - when you reach the tarmac road go left to reach the house.

From here there is a magnificent view of the lake, and a path by a bench and sign bears right back deep into the woods. Follow the red waymarks, now leading down to another foot-bridge and through young woodland before descending to another bridge, keeping straight ahead to a little bench with a viewpoint, by a little picture-shrine among the trees. The path descends once again into another gully, twisting down and across the shallow valley. Ignore a crossing path but keep to a wire fence straight ahead, the path soon reaching a handsome bridge over the Dexelbach.

At the next junction of paths keep straight ahead - fine views are to be enjoyed again across to the lake from this path. You cross yet another bridge and follow a cool green way through woods, across a meadow and by a corn field before going back into the wood and turning left into a steep tarmac lane.

Bear left here, climbing some 80 metres uphill along the lane before bearing right along a path signed to Nußdorf which soon reaches a road by a farm. Turn right here and follow the road gently descending for some 200 metres to where, just past cottages, the West Wanderweg branches off left at a track into the wood - look for signs. This becomes a path now zig-zagging steeply uphill just inside the wood before reaching a broader path. Turn right here, descending by a stream to another crossroads. Keep right again downhill by the stream to a rather complex crossing point above a ravine. Your way is the main path downhill, keeping the same direction, down the spine of what is a low ridge, by an old streambed which soon becomes a broad path by a stream into the outskirts of Nußdorf - a scattered lakeside resort.

Keep ahead past Gasthöfe and houses to the main road. Almost opposite a quiet street - Bachgasse - continues to follow the stream before becoming a field path by campsites and lakeside recreational areas until you reach the lido and landing stages where you'll have time to check your return boat times and find refreshment. Drinks and light snacks are also available on board the boat.

WALK THIRTEEN: ALMSEE - 11km (6½ miles) Easy

Starting and Finishing Point: Bus stop at Gasthof Jagersimmerl, at the junction with the Odensee Road, Almtal. Alternatively, a return can be made by catching the bus back from the Almsee terminus (6km).

This can be reached by taking Postbus 2554 direct from Gmunden via Scharnstein and Grünau, but services are limited to the main holiday months with variations between Sundays and weekdays and Saturdays - careful timetable reading required. But the basic morning, midday and afternoon return service can, with careful planning, not only make this ramble perfectly convenient, but can be combined with a visit to the Cumberland Wildlife Park passed en route.

There is a öBB train service from Wels as far as Grünau (Table 15b).

Motorists: Car park at the road junction with the Odensee Road.

Refreshments: Jagersimmerl; Almsee - Seehaus and Deutsches Haus.

Major Attractions: Grünau village, the Almsee; the Cumberland Wildlife Park.

Map: Wanderkarte 19 Almtal-Kremstal-Steyrtal

Almtal forms the eastern boundary of the Salzkammergut which because of its distance from popular tourist routes gets relatively few British visitors. It is of great charm, a richly fertile valley of scattered communities, thickly forested above Grünau and, at its head, a magnificent jewel, the Almsee itself, so perfectly set against the towering peaks of the Totes Gebirge mountains. This little known part of the Salzkammergut offers great possibilities for anyone who loves wild and unspoiled places.

The Cumberland Wildlife Park in Almtal, is in the former estates of the last Duke of Cumberland (*d.* 1923 - son of King George V of Hanover). This is a superbly set and exceptionally interesting 'wild park' - semi-natural open air zoo - associated

Almtal - Almsee and the Totes Gebirge

with the work of the internationally famous zoologist Konrad Lorenz. It is devoted to Alpine mammals and birds. (Light refreshments available.) A visit to the Wildlife Park, (bus stop outside the gates) can be combined with this walk on the current Salzkammergut Postbus timetable.

The Almsee is also outstanding for its bird life - wild geese and swans in particular, and a 'floating island' built from vegetation which moves around the lake depending on weather conditions and lake levels.

Alight from the bus and walk about 100 metres along the Odensee Road crossing the River Alm, immediately after which turn right along a track by an old watermill. The path soon enters a wood of tall fir trees. Follow the signs to Almsee. Bear left over a footbridge over a side stream, continuing through a lovely stretch of woodland and a low headland before descending to the lakeside near Schwarzenbrunn where a bridge over the river at the foot of the lake provides a fine view along the lake.

Keep to the path along the riverside which rapidly broadens into the full expanse of lake, the views getting ever more impressive, with the craggy summits of the Totes Gebirge now reflected in the shimmering waters. The central peak of the range, directly ahead, is the Zwölferkogel (2,033m).

This is an easy to follow path along the lakeside past the odd boat-house or fisherman's hut, the views ever more perfect, a photographer's delight. As you approach the head of the lake fresh springs bubble into the lake from the shore, and the path curves round over low-lying ground and crosses the Aagbach by a wooden bridge to reach two restaurants - the Seehaus and the excellent Deutches Haus, the latter offering a number of specialist traditional Austrian and Salzkammergut recipes to delight the gourmet's - and the walker's - heart.

To make a circular walk you can either follow the main road along the east shore of the lakeside to Schwarzenbrunn - except for Sundays and main holiday periods it is relatively quiet being a cul-de-sac - or take one of the forest tracks back to Schwarzenbrunn, though care will be needed as there is a choice of routes and not all are waymarked. From Schwarzenbrunn cross the footbridge back to path 404 to return to Jagersimmerl.

However, there is much to be said for retracing your steps along the entirety of that delectable woodland way from the top of the valley.

There might be even more to recommend, if the weather is fine, merely enjoying the rest of the afternoon in such surroundings before catching the late afternoon Postbus (check times carefully) back down Almtal to Grünau and Gmunden.

APPENDIX

SOME USEFUL WORDS AND PHRASES FOR RAMBLERS

For non-German speaking ramblers we have compiled a brief list of some of the more common words and phrases you're likely to meet or need in the Austrian Salzkammergut. For those with some knowledge of German, you will find that basically apart from some terms for the more common foods, there is little difference from standard German terminology.

On The Route

High pasture - also farm with refreshments	der Alm
High-level path	der Höhenweg
Footpath	der Füssweg/Füsspfad
A climb (footpath)	der Steig
Glacier	der Gletscher
Farm track	der Wirtschaftsweg
Road	die Strasse/Gasse
Forest Path	der Waldweg
Meadow, field	die Wiese
Steps	die Treppe/Stiege
Mountain (dome-shaped)	der Kogel
No Entry	Eintritt Verboten
Danger	Achtung Lebensgefährlich!
Take Care!	Bitte Vorsicht!
Rock fall	der Steinschlag, die Lawine
Map	die Landkarte
River	der Fluss
Lake	der See
Bridge	die Brücke
Local Museum	das Heimatmuseum
Monastry	das Kloster/Stift
Parish church	die Pfarrkirche
Pilgrimage church	die Wallfahrtskirche
Swimming Pool	das Hallenbad
Open Air Swimming Pool	das Freibad
Tourist Information	der Fremdenverkersamt
Post Office	der Postamt

Postage Stamp	die Briefmarke
Postcard	die Postkarte
Holiday	der Urlaub
Summer holidays (in the country)	die Sommerfrische
Good morning	Gruß Gott!
Please....	Bitte
Thank you	Danke schön
Excuse me....	Entschuldigen Sie mir bitte...
Do you speak English?	Sprechen Sie Englisch?
I don't understand	Ich verstehe nicht
Please speak more slowly	Bitte, sprechen Sie noch langsamer
I am lost	Ich habe mich verirrt
Can you help me?	Können Sie mir helfen?
How far is it to....	Wie weit ist es von hier nach....?
Is this the way to....?	Ist das der Weg nach....?
Straight on	Gerade aus
Left	Links
Right	Rechts
Close the gate	Gatter schliessen

Accommodation

Rooms	Zimmer
Rooms to let, vacancies	Zimmer frei
Bed	das Bett
Shower	die Dusche
Bath	das Bad
Breakfast	das Frühstück
Dinner	das Abendessen
Lunch	das Mittagessen
Toilets	die Toiletten, der Abort, das Klo (more colloquial, '00')
Ladies	Damen
Gentlemen	Herren
Vacant	Frei
Occupied	Besetzt
Lift	der Fahrstuhl, Lift
Telephone	das Telefon
to Telephone	anrufen
I have reserved a room	Ich habe ein Zimmer reserviert
What time is breakfast?	Um wieviel Uhr wird das Früstück serviert?
Breakfast is from....to....	Das Frühstück ist von....bis....
What time is it?	Wie spät ist es?
Is this seat/place free?	Bitte, ist der Platz/Sitz frei?

No, this seat is taken   Nein, der Platz ist reserviert
Yes, it's free   Ja, bitte sehr

Food and Drink

Meal	das Essen
Menu	die Karte
Soup	die Suppe
Gamesoup	die Wildsuppe
Beef	das Rindfleisch
Rissoles	die Fleischlaibchen
Roast Pork	der Schweinsbraten
Chicken	das Huhn, Hendl
Turkey	der Truthahn/Putan/Indian
Venison	das Reh, der Hirsch (braten)
Boiled Egg	gekochtes Ei
Fish	der Fisch
Hake	der Dorsch
Char	der Saibling
Trout	die Forelle
Salmon	der Lachs
Veal	das Kalb
Bread	das Brot
Bread Roll	die Semmel
Milk	die Milch
Cheese	der Käse
Ice-cream	das Eis
Beer	das Bier
Tea	der Tee
Coffee	der Kaffee
Water	das Wasser
Mineral water	das Mineralwasser
Apple (grape, orange) juice	Apfel (Trauben, Orangen) saft
Wine	der Wein
Cream	der Schlagobers
with cream	mit Schlag
Butter	die Butter
Sugar	der Zucher
Salt	das Salz
Cauliflower	der Karfiol/Blumenkohl
Tomato	die Tomate/Paradieser
Carrot	die Karotte
Spinach	der Spinat
French beans	die Fisolen, die Grüne Bohnen
Gherkins	die Gurken
Potatoes	die Kartoffeln, Erdäpfel
Green Salad	der Kopfsalat

APPENDIX - USEFUL WORDS
APPENDIX - USEFUL WORDS
APPENDIX - USEFUL WORDS

Mixed Salad	Gemischter Salat
Mushrooms	die Pilze
Mushrooms (Chanterelles)	die Eierschwammerl
Apricots	die Marillen
Bilberries	die Heidelbeeren
Cranberries	die Preiselbeeren
Red currants	die Riebisel
Plums	die Zwetschken, Pflaumen
Cake	der Kuchen
Gateau	die Torte
Crescent-shaped pastries or rolls	die Kipferl
Pasta	die Nudeln
Dumplings	die Knödel
Chocolate	die Schokolade
Cake and pastry shop	die Konditorei
Did you enjoy the meal?	Hat Ihnen das Essen geschmeckt?
Yes, very much	Ja, sehr!
The bill	Die Rechnung, bitte Zahlen!

Transport

Train	der Zug - die Bahn
Express train	der Schnellzug
Stopping train	der Eilzug, Personenzug
Cable-car railway	die Seilbahn
Chair-lift	der Sesselbahn
Bus	der Autobus
Bus stop	die Autobus Haltstelle
Journey	die Fahrt/Reise
Ticket	die Fahrkarte
Single	Einfach
Return	Hin-und-Zurück
Luggage	das Gepäck
Platform	der Bahnsteig or der Gleis (bay)
To change trains	umsteigen
No smoking	Nicht rauchen
Timetable	der Fahrplan
Departures	Abfahrt
Arrivals	Ankunft
What is the fare to....?	Wieviel kostet es nach....?
From which platform does it leave?	Von welchen Bahnsteig fährt er?
Airport	der Flughafen
One-way street	Einbahn
Taxi	das Taxi
Petrol	das Benzin

Diesel (oil)	das Diesel
Bank	die Sparkasse
Passport	der Reisepass
Currency changing	Geldwächsel
Travellers cheques	die Reisechecks
Doctor	der Arzt
Dentist	der Zahnarzt
Pain	Schmerzen
Hospital	das Krankenhaus/Spittal
Nurse	die Krankenschwester
Ambulance	der Krankenwagen
Accident	der Unfall
Insurance	die Versicherung
Police	die Polizei
Help	Hilfe!
Lost	Verloren
Stolen	Gestohlen
I have a toothache	Ich habe Zahnweh
Hayfever	der Heuschnupfen
A cold	der Schnupfen
Headache	die Kopfschmerzen, das Kopfweh
Stomach ache	die Magenschmerzen
Heart attack	das Herzanfall
Diabetes	die Zuckerkrankheit, der Diabetes
Allergy	die Allergie
Sunburn	der Sonnenbrand
Sickness, nausea	die Übelkeit
Blister	die Blase
A sprained (ankle, knee)	(der Knöchel, das Knie) verstauchen
Elastoplast, sticking plaster	das Pflaster
Chemist's shop	die Apotheke

FURTHER READING

Although there is little in English directly on the Salzkammergut itself apart from some fairly smallish sections in some of the better known guides, there are numerous splendidly illustrated books often with minimal text or even English captions available in Austria to whet the appetite.

Stella Musulin's *Austria: People and Landscape* published by Faber 1971 gives a lively account (albeit with a post-war flavour) of particular aspects of the country as a whole, especially some of its more colourful historical figures and there is an interesting section on the Salzkammergut in the Upper Austria chapter.

The *Merian* guides in German are full of splendid illustrations with well researched articles and information on many different aspects of the cultural and historical heritage in the area. Many useful travel tips etc. are also included. But Merian's *Salzkammergut* and *Ober Osterreich* (Upper Austria) are only for those with a good knowledge of German.

For those who are particularly interested in the Emperor Franz Joseph's connections with Ischl *Ischl unter Kaiser Franz Joseph I* by Caroline Markolin and Peter Huemer (available at the Kaiservilla in Ischl) gives a detailed scholarly insight into that relationship with some excellent period photographs.

There are numerous biographies of the Emperor Franz Joseph I and Empress Elisabeth both in German and also in English; many take a highly romantic view of the famous couple, but are great fun to read.

Finally, virtually all places of interest provide attractive brochures either in an English language version or with a perfectly adequate English summary.

*Printed by CARNMOR PRINT & DESIGN
LONDON ROAD, PRESTON, LANCASHIRE*